# Classless

Recent Essays on British Film

# Classless

Recent Essays on British Film

## Carl Neville

BOOKS

Winchester, UK
Washington, USA

First published by O-Books, 2011
O Books is an imprint of John Hunt Publishing Ltd., The Bothy, Deershot Lodge, Park Lane, Ropley,
Hants, SO24 0BE, UK
office1@o-books.net
www.o-books.com

For distributor details and how to order please visit the 'Ordering' section on our website.

Text copyright: Carl Neville 2010

ISBN: 978 1 84694 380 5

A CIP catalogue record for this book is available from the British Library.

Design: Tom Davies

Printed in the UK by CPI Antony Rowe
Printed in the USA by Offset Paperback Mfrs, Inc

We operate a distinctive and ethical publishing philosophy in all
areas of its business, from its global network of authors to
production and worldwide distribution.

# CONTENTS

# Introduction

Anybody attempting to write even a short book on recent British film will rapidly discover that there is much to be endured, little to be enjoyed. This book takes the films of Danny Boyle as its main subject, partly because they have been both critically and commercially successful, partly because they span the Major through Blair to Brown years.

In the past fifteen years, I have watched British film attempting to assert its Britishness, but I have found that the terrain it maps out seems wholly foreign to my own experience. Largely this felt like someone else's cinema, or rather a cinema functioning almost exclusively as PR for the notion of that New Modern Britain every successive government has offered up and failed to deliver.

There are of course all kinds of systemic pressures on the film industry in the UK which determine the kinds of films that have been and can be made, but these won't be examined here. *Classless* is more concerned with identifying the ideological character of recent British cinema, the ways in which it is tied into the dominant neoliberal orthodoxies of Blairism, (*Trainspotting, The Beach*) and ways in which it reacts against them (*Orphans, Adam and Paul*), how it adapts as the media and celebrity reach saturation point, co-opting other forms of expression (*The Queen, Slumdog Millionaire*). *Classless* also finds in the popular sub-genre of Hooligan films (*Football Factory, The Firm, Rise of the Footsoldiers* and others) the potential for a more critical cinema. Finally we examine the ambiguous possibilities for transformation offered up by Lynne Ramsay's *Morvern Caller* and Glazier's *Sexy Beast*.

## Trainspotting *and beyond*

The film which came to define the mid to late nineties in the UK and set the style and tone for almost everything that followed was Danny Boyle's *Trainspotting* (1996). A highly stylized rendering of Irvine Welsh's scabrous cult novel of the same name, it was recently voted the best British film of the past twenty-five years in a poll in *The Observer*.

The novel was first published in 1993, the year after the Conservative party, under John Major, had been returned to office. Despite being elected with a substantial majority, the victory was still widely regarded as a surprise. Major was the gray man of British politics, an avuncular, nondescript figure, especially in comparison to his strident, polarizing and increasingly unpopular predecessor Margaret Thatcher. The most important British films of 1992 and 1993 were, commercially, Merchant Ivory's handsome adaptation of E. M. Forster, *Howard's End*, and artistically (in terms of their reception at Cannes) two films by long-standing British realists: Mike Leigh's *Naked* and Ken Loach's *Raining Stones*.

These films, glossy heritage cinema on the one hand and low-budget social-realist on the other, represented the two dominant traditions of British cinema at the time. In both Britain and the US, the impact of Quentin Tarantino's dynamic, gritty heist movie *Reservoir Dogs* in 1992 and his slicker, more overtly postmodern *Pulp Fiction* (1994) was immense. Here was a witty and pop-culture literate film-maker whose hip and hyperkinetic style made not just most British films seem stuffy and staid, but outdid formulaic big-budget Hollywood in crowd-pleasing thrills too.

An emerging set of young filmmakers looked to Tarantino's flair and panache as a way of revitalizing a stale national cinema. During the mid-nineties, there was a sense that a change of government was inevitable, that in the next election the Tories would finally lose. This came to pass in 1997, although what appeared to be a dramatic change was in many ways simply a continuation: much of New Labour's rhetoric and many of their policies once in power can be traced back to John Major's more concerned, caring Conservatism. The change actually amounted to only a change in style. Rather as emerging British filmmakers like Danny Boyle looked across the Atlantic to Tarantino and the wave of smart, young "indie" filmmakers (Hal Hartley, Whit Stillman, John Dahl), so too the Labour Party visited the states to pick up electioneering tips from the Clinton campaign.

Already in the early nineties there was much talk of a classless society: indeed it was one of Major's avowed aims to create just such a thing. The great international success of British cinema in the Major years' was Richard Curtis' *Four Weddings and Funeral* (1994), which portrays an idealized England in which groups of posh, bright young things, only nominally drawn from a variety of backgrounds, gad about an England filled with Heritage properties and roomy flats. Curtis's vision of England, immensely popular both at home and abroad, represented a comforting shift back to an Evelyn Waugh Thirties of Bright Young Things and mild domestic comedy, a welcome antidote to the bitterness, pessimism and anger against Thatcherism that had characterized much of the filmmaking of the eighties. The return to the Thirties as exemplified by *Four Weddings* and Branagh's *Peter's Friends* (1992) would itself soon be supplanted by the comparatively more youthful return to the sixties brought about by the shift away from the New Man toward Lad Culture and the emergence of Cool Britannia, a response to the domination of the UK music scene by American retro-rock in the wake of Nirvana's phenomenal success with *Nevermind*.

New Lads were presented as more pleasure-orientated, traditionally "male" and responsibility-shy antidote to the New Man. New Men were feminized, caring and sharing, well-groomed, emotionally expressive, while New Laddism was an ironic take on what were perceived as the core male pleasures: drinking in the company of other men, chasing girls, going to the football, not changing your socks. This is a particular perception of working class culture rebranded as "lifestyle", "lad" being, after all, a colloquial working class term to describe young men.

There is an emphasis on honesty in both the New Man and the New Lad, though with the latter it is a harsh insistence on how men "really feel" regarding gender issues and sex as opposed to the former's openness about his emotions, fears and hopes. In the film adaptation of *About a Boy* (2002), for example Hugh Grant, in New Lad mode, turns down the offer to become godfather to a friend's child on the basis that when she reaches eighteen he'll probably just take her out, get her drunk and "try to shag her". A part of the New Lad's appeal is his scandalizing honesty about how men are. In this way New Laddism presents itself as a "real" against the pretentiousness and phoniness of the New Man.

The leading exponent of Lad Culture in the UK was the magazine Loaded (launched in 1994), which emphasized birds, booze, footy and mildly shocking, unreconstructed attitudes. Loaded continued the targeting of men as consumers that had begun a few years earlier, in the late eighties, with the establishment of more "serious" magazines such as GQ and Esquire. With their emphasis on the consumption of expensive commodities, professionalism and quality journalism, the target audience was smart young professionals who cared about grooming. The launch of Loaded was an attempt to tap into a sector of society that falls outside the "yuppie" demographic but still has money to spend.

Lad Culture tied into some of the other significant areas of rebranding in the early nineties, one of which was the "gentrification" of football. This was undertaken as a way of attracting higher earners as customers and removing the hooligan element that had blighted the game during the eighties. Football began to lose its class and gender connotations, became family-friendly and, with the rise of the super celebrity footballer, more glamorous. Losing its specific class connotations it becomes primarily, but not exclusively, a "boys" pursuit. *Fever Pitch* (1996) is about a middle-class man's obsession with Arsenal and how it affects his relationship. Through the late eighties and on into the early nineties, retail and services became the most important sectors of the UK economy; shopping becomes the main pastime, and pubs start to be adapted into middle-class leisure spaces (Gastropubs, etc). Rave culture had ushered in a significantly more relaxed attitude to drugs among all classes and the early nineties see the emergence of Superclubs, comodifying much of rave's outlaw energy.

The New Lad has been directly targeted by and represented in British film, relatively slowly at first, but now there is a micro-industry of straight-to-DVD features devoted to him. Most early considerations of the subject were, as in the adaptations of Nick Hornby's novels *Fever Pitch*, *High Fidelity* and *About a Boy*, attempts to position the New Man as the inevitable destiny for the New Lad: his extended adolescence will eventually resolve itself into a rueful acceptance of family and monogamy. But there is also a genre of films drawing on both the British gangster movie and the New Lad/ New Man films mentioned above which offer the possibility of a more critically engaged cinema. The Football Hooligan film begins in 1992 with Phil Daniels' *I.D.*, while the most recent addition to the genre is Nick Love's remake of Alan Clarke's seminal TV piece *The Firm*.

Two much-disputed, but still highly influential ideas, which will be central to this book, are "The end of History" and the "Nairn-Anderson thesis". The idea of the end of History derives from Francis Fukuyama's *The End of History and the Last Man*. Essentially, Fukuyama posits the global dominance of liberal democracy as the terminus of historical development. With the collapse of the USSR, it appeared that capitalism had won the ideological battle as the best provider of "equal recognition under the law". At the End of History, there may still be inequalities in wealth and opportunity, but in principle everyone has equal status in the eyes of the law. There is no serious progressive challenger to liberal democracy; individual status needs are to be managed by consumerism. This idea gained common currency throughout the nineties and was tirelessly repeated: capitalism isn't perfect but it's the best system we have, or can have.

The Nairn-Anderson thesis – named after the two theorists who developed it, Tom Nairn and Perry Anderson – underpins two of the most substantial works of British Cinema in the past twenty years, Patrick Keiller's *London* (1994) and *Robinson in Space* (1997), in which the narrator sets out to anatomize "the problem of England". The problem is England's singular relationship to modernity, or perhaps its singular inability to achieve modernity in the European manner. "The failure of the English revolution is all around us," Keiller's Robinson muses at one point: England's revolution has come too early, leaving much the deep structure of the class system intact and merely glossing over it with a shallow constitutionalism. England is caught in an unresolved tension between its apparent modernity and the reality of its deeply embedded semi-feudal social relations. It is this unresolved tension and the inability to really grasp the nettle of what is necessary for genuine social change in England (i.e. a restaging of the Revolution that failed) that fuels much of the rage that underpins English life just as it fuels the fantasy, especially exaggerated in the early nineties and under New Labour, that somehow the class system can be wished, or better still shopped, away. As I write, with England still caught up in recession after the banking crisis and a general election pending, class as a political issue seems to be returning from exile. The Rage will be considered later, but we'll begin with the Fantasy. Just as there is "irrational exuberance" in economic matters, a phrase coined by Alan Greenspan to describe the speculative frenzy that is instrumental in building up financial bubbles, there is also a political and cultural form of irrational exuberance: the rush to believe that what is being offered up does represent a genuine change, that this time there really will be a restitution and fulfillment of the promises made, that we have entered a new age, no longer bedeviled by the past. And just as the affective cycle that characterizes financial bubbles ends in distress and revulsion, so too in the other spheres of life. The nineties through the noughties in the UK represent just such a bubble in the cultural stock of all things keen simultaneously to assert their modernity and their Britishness.

# 1. Smackhead Millionaires: *Trainspotting*

## The constitution of the addressee

Just such exuberance might be found in Danny Boyle and John Hodge's *Trainspotting*. In its speediness and its euphoria, *Trainspotitng's* aesthetic is more akin to the effects of Ecstasy or cocaine than heroin. Here, Ewan McGregor's Renton is the fantasy projection of the Poorist middle classes, representing a brief, invigorating holiday in transgression from which they can return replete with all kinds of subcultural capital: the clothes, the drugs, the music, the bars, the terminology. The Information. Poverty and "social exclusion" are aesthetic and discursive playgrounds: being a junkie doesn't mean you can't look good or riff on pop culture in a knowing way. No need to mourn anything or wring your hands over anyone's lots, because everybody is having, as a book title of the time put it, *Adventures in Capitalism*.

If *Trainspotting* represents an attempt to elide the working classes by positing an urban pastoral, it's one in which underclass energy and savvy feeds directly into middle-class narcissism. *Trainspotting's* return to the sixties, its Beatles referencing and by extension its Cool Britannia/Brit-Pop stylization, attempts a temporal elision of the bitter Seventies and combative Eighties, back to the last time England could reasonably have been said to be "sexy", where class seemed momentarily a mirage and the prospect of brave new heterotopias spun giddily on the horizon. After all, with the abandoning of Clause Four which had committed the Labour Party to National ownership of key industries, a new form of postwar consensus emerged: There Is No Alternative. "The working class are such a disappointment," as Kureshi and Frears' *My Beautiful Laundrette* (1985) reminded us, whereas the underclass are just so mouth-wateringly dynamic and unthreateningly unorganized.

It's not simply that cheeky Brit-pop skaghead Renton finally decides, through some mysterious neoliberal alchemy, to choose life and thereby affirm, if not all the stultifying choices he rejects at the start in favor of smack, then at least a lifestyle of high consumerism, "a fucking big telly" (with the lascivious " fucking" emphasizing his libidinized more-Consumerist-than-thou new hyper-Realism). It's rather that Renton IS the middle class audience member herself, leaping as though through force of sheer magical yearning into the frame and the film's world and eventually with a knowing, conspiratorial wink, melting back out of it to rejoin herself at the end. The permeability of the screen, the looking glass through which the viewer passes, is the fantasy of the permeability of social barriers in the newly classless, New Labour Britain.

This is part of the film's obsession with choice and it's casting of poverty as something which one can opt in or out of at will, bridging the gap between underclass smack-addiction and the world of big TVs at one existential stroke. Poverty is a consequence of individual lack of graft or get-up-and-go, cozily reaffirming to the gap year and trust-fund brigade that a few years of chemical romance can easily be set aside when the time comes to re-join the real world you were only ever having a little vacation from anyway.

Indeed, in much of Boyle's work there is no social or psychological fixity: for the protean middle classes at least, everything is fluid and opt-into and out-able. In *Shallow Grave*, *28 Days Later* and *The Beach*, psychopathology is also a temporary state, exploited as required in order to get the job done, just one more weapon in the armory of late capitalist character traits. The primal savage is always there just below the surface, handily allowing, for example, the wispy Cillian Murphy to wipe out an entire platoon of soldiers in *28 Days Later*.

One of the fantasies these films gratify is the viewer's desire to be a complete subject, a subject who is capable of anything and, who knows, who has experienced everything: on the one hand grounded, responsible, "realistic", capable of making the right "choices"; on the other hand secretly exultant in their belief that they are the culmination of history.

Hipsterism, of which *Trainspotting* is an early example, is the assumption on the part of the middle class subject that there is no position which they cannot occupy, that both class and identity politics have been overcome, or at least that class has been subsumed into identity. The middle class assumes a kind of transcendent, post-historical emptiness into which all cultures can be incorporated. While others are bounded by ethnicity, class, gender – they are limited entities, with a finite set of facets and characteristics – the hipster is capable of endlessly moving between different lifestyle options.

*Trainspotting*'s ethic and aesthetic are a further extension and deepening of the American ethos, so ably represented by Curtis Hanson's *Eight Mile* (2002), that marshaling a set of given proletarian skills – linguistic flair, a cultural capital of realness, soul and more-than-rugged individualism bordering on sociopathy – will allow you to prevail if and only if the individual is ready. In the state of late capitalist precariousness, readiness is all. "Opportunity comes once in a lifetime," Eminem's "Release Yourself" tells us; you will have your chance, if you blow it you know who's to blame: not the system which democratically allocates an opportunity to all, but the individual. *Trainspotting's* relation to the series of Brit Films (*Little Voice, Billy Elliot, The Full Monty*) will have to be teased out elsewhere, but suffice to say: if you can't sing or dance then there's always crime.

Renton's escape is via a drug deal set up and orchestrated by others, his apparent friends, who he then rips off, except for the guileless Spud, who unlike Begbie and Sick Boy is in need of a bit of charity. It doesn't matter how you get the money, the important thing is that you put a bit back, offering alms for the deserving poor. Spud's discovery of the money in the locker in the film's coda is the final attempt to absolve Renton/ the viewer. This is how you get out of poverty, crime or culture. You may need to ditch your friends along the way: so much for all that sharing of scores and junk camaraderie, so much for solidarity, so much for refusal. At the end of the day, when the opportunity comes, you choose life and comfortingly affirm the conservatism you attacked in your youth.

This is how to live in Cool Britannia.

As the knowledge economy gears up, as London becomes the center of finance, as a young, sexy, globalized Britain prepares to start up, and the boom years of cheap credit, massive personal debt, seemingly ever-rising house prices and an economy organized around orgiastic consumption and compulsory positivity are about to kick in, we might be tempted to a more chastening conclusion than even early sixties/mid-nineties archetype Arthur Seaton, the central character of *Saturday Night and Sunday Morning* (1960) managed.

A good time can also be a form of propaganda.

### Welshian heroism

In his cameo in *Trainspotting* Irvine Welsh is wearing an Exploited t-shirt, but despite this seeming advocacy the band are noticeably missing from the film's soundtrack, which is comprised of "cutting edge" Britpop tracks by the likes of Blur and Sleeper, a smattering of techno and some middlebrow classics by Iggy and Eno. The lumpen antagonism of The Exploited is too alienating and alienated, too politicized, to soundtrack the onscreen hi-jinks and bright-eyed enthusiasm for heroin addiction. Nonetheless, Welsh feels the need to wear it, a pennant of his deathless allegiance to/knowledge of a punk underground nowhere else glimpsed in the film.

A part of The Exploited's micro-mystique is that they were one of the bands, along with Conflict, Discharge and the Subhumans, who took punk away from its co-option by the mainstream, into a subaltern world of anarchist commitment. They weren't fashionable, they weren't post-punk in any of its currently understood senses, there were very few major labels sniffing round them, and even if they were, their politics demanded that they would tell them to fuck off. The Exploited signified a kind of anti-plastic-punk Real.

Yet in an essay Welsh published at the time, reprinted as part of the ten year anniversary DVD of *Trainspotting*, in which among other things he defends the decision to shoot *Trainspotting* in a non-realist fashion, he can name someone like Liam Gallagher as a working class hero. From Welsh's perspective Liam is a working class hero not because he has directly done anything for/with the working class but precisely because he's got away from it. He represents the working class not through any specific set of political positions – class politics having been, after all, relegated to the dustbin of history – but through his "attitude", his mad-for-it hedonism, his straight talking, his punch ups, his mocking sarcasm, all nicely combined with his reverence for an unthreatening resurgent strand of contemporary Heritage culture, namely The Beatles.

Heroism, you would think, entailed some potential danger to – or sacrifice made by – the putative hero, some risk-taking: where is the heroism in getting rich and buying a mansion on the basis of a few mild épaterings of the bourgeoisie plus Trad-rock? The novel's most effective advocate for this position is Sick Boy, in his rejection of the attachments and allegiances of old Labour and the Victorian stridency of Thatcherism. "The socialists go on about your comrades, your class, your union and society. Fuck all that shite. The Tories go on about your employer, your country, your family. Fuck that even mair. It's me, me, fucking me."

Working class heroism is Liam Gallagher's heroism, as opposed to the evident non-heroism of defeated, uncool relics of the past like Scargill. With *Trainspotting* Welsh in no way changes the world he writes about, but somehow, by heroically reporting on it, representing it, raising it from invisibility into consciousness, better still into "coolness", he has fulfilled his duty. In a post-Historical scenario, in which the conservative notion of recognition rather than any dangerously disruptive notions of equality are in the ascendant, then coolness is perhaps the greatest, if not only, gift to be bestowed upon the subaltern classes.

### Non-realist naturalization
The decision not to make *Trainspotting* in the well established British realist tradition was made, according to producer Andrew MacDonald, on the basis that cinema is about the "imagination". Welsh asserts that realist forms patronize their working class subjects. Non-realist treatments, however, don't moralize or portray the lives of addicts as wretched; this is the service they render that group's particular "choice". This is the underlying assumption of the film: that heroin addiction is a choice. Ironically, though, it is *Trainspotting*'s non-realist mode that serves to naturalize the notion of heroin use as an

individual choice. Non-realism can also be thoroughly in the service of the dominant ideology. In fact, with *Trainspotting*, the bolder and more subversive choice, the choice that cut against the grain of Third Way tolerance, would have been a stridently politicized, thoroughly traditional realism. The problem not only of Hodge's script but also of Boyle's style gapes open at the end of Renton's first monologue, opening up the aporia into which the whole project stumbles. "I chose not to choose life. I chose something else. And the reasons? (pause) There are no reasons. Who needs reasons when you've got heroin?"

The rushed, half-fumbled delivery of the lines after the pause, the film's stupidly setting itself a question it then can't answer, represent the crux of *Trainspotting*'s failure: its inability to provide anything other than a glossy rush that masks any deeper consideration as to why from the mid-eighties onward Heroin use might have steadily grown to become pandemic across Scotland and in the former industrial heartland of England itself. There are no reasons, no wider forces shape you, you choose or you don't, and any way, heroin relieves you of the burden of questioning. The opposition between a non-judgmental imaginative rendering and a patronizing realism assumes that that in some way McDonald, Boyle and Hodge are more on the side of the underclass by representing them as attractive, even enviable, rather than suffering and pitiable.

Welsh's complaint is that in realism the poor are being presented as victims (but the poor *are* victims); that they will be portrayed as divested of agency (but the poor have been divested of agency). We precisely don't patronize the underclass, in this view, when we confer upon them the notion that they share in our middle class subjectivity, which also presents itself as the universal subjectivity.

The ideological cast of this mindset, the extension of

Welsh's much more ambivalent "Smart Cunt" who will stick to drugs to get him through the long, dark night of late capitalism, is worth exploring, but the film doesn't have the intelligence to do so. The vaunted "imagination" evident here has been co-opted from MTV, Tarantino and Scorsese, especially *Goodfellas* (1990), and the ways in which all of these may be extensions of Richard Lester's work with The Beatles. A quick comparison of the start of *A Hard Day's Night* (1964) – in which The Beatles are pursued by screaming fans as the title track plays – with *Trainspotting* will assure you that Boyle knows how to set up his rock and roll archetypes via the mythic force of voice over and the freeze frame. The exciting, new British cinema will express itself through the visual tropes of American postmodernism. Cool Britannia will return to the sixties via Tarantino's *Reservoir Dogs*, itself a return to and an instantiation of the notion that the early seventies is the Golden Age of American cinema.

### The living and the dead
There are two deaths in *Trainspotting*. There's the baby, and the minor character Tommy, who dies of toxoplasmosis.

Tommy is coded from the start as a naïf, his angelic mop of blond hair and wide-eyed expression mark him out as a wimpily uxorious holy innocent who foolishly gets into smack when his girlfriend leaves him over a missing sex video they've made together, one Renton has stolen for a few minutes passing amusement. Renton also introduces him to smack and therefore his later death is directly attributable to him.

Tommy's problem from the start, which causes Renton's initial reluctance to let him get involved, is that he's just not tough enough for smack: he's too straight, too lacking in the constitutional cool of Renton and Sick Boy who are ontologically fit-for-purpose for the rollercoaster of smack addiction.

Tommy can't handle his drugs. In some ways he becomes a pitiable figure, with his inability to get out of bed, his emotional need for the kitten whose shit finally kills him, his sulky, recriminatory face in Renton's cold-turkey nightmare. Tommy is a failure as a smackhead and his failure, his inadequacy, resides in his emotionalism. His funeral is a perfunctory affair, a drag from which Renton escapes to go and score, death and funerals representing an unwelcome interruption in the round of copping, shooting, kicking and hustling. Funerals and death force you to have to interact with the square world of parents, the uncool world of grief. Renton and Sick boy can take the punishment. In the brutal political economy of smack there are winners and losers, and there's little doubt that if you can handle smack you can handle anything. The film doesn't care about Tommy, why should it, he's not one of the new people on new drugs the film lionizes, he's an old-school loser. To survive in late capitalism you have to have a high tolerance for toxicity, low levels of emotional need.

The fantasy of toughness, the rhetoric of toughness: neoliberalism is an adult's discipline, demanding an autonomous maturity of its subjects; life is a proving ground, the market a furnace of purgative struggle in which the dross will be melted away. While the rhetoric is softened in the Blairite Third Way, taking on a tone of exasperatedly crusading realism, in the less guarded political climate of the US, neoliberal hawks are often to be found castigating the immaturity the welfare state induces and moralizing about the pitiful dependence and lack of frontier spirit found in European economies. At this point of course Britain is being held up as the modern, European economy par excellence because of its swingeing cuts in public spending, its promotion of business and the increasingly unregulated financial institutions that will transform the white elephant of

Canary Wharf into the world center for finance (leaving Blairism to concentrate on its own empty monument to hubris, the Millennium Dome, just across the river). Those who cannot survive in the neoliberal marketplace are half-subjects, untermenshen, still clinging feebly to the skirts of the state. Pampered, indulged, spoiled, mummy's boys. There is only one true model of human subjectivity and that is the completely self-reliant entrepreneur, the highest expression of capitalism. Now free-market capitalism has come out on top, the Last Man is a kind of god, the incarnation of historical and human truth. Those societies in which there are still atavistic welfare structures and mixed economies are backward, peopled by contemptible overgrown babies who must be beaten into a responsible adulthood, who must have their toys, minimum wages, unions, free health care, generous pensions, taken away.

# 2. The Correctives:
## *Orphans, Adam and Paul*

There are two films which stand on either side of *Trainspotting* and shame its lack of political courage, visual flair and wit. The first of these is Peter Mullan's *Orphans* (1997).

If *Trainspotting* glorifies a new kind of rugged individualism, then *Orphans* is prepared to make an explicit connection between the death of Socialism and the loss of a sheltering parent. Many of the themes in *Orphans* are prefigured in Mullen's superb trio of short films, especially *The Fridge* (1995), a nightmare vision – seemingly compounded from Beckett's *Play* and Lynch's *Eraserhead* – of the destitution and impoverishment of the Scottish working classes, of the terrible social atomization, fear and addiction that will condemn a child to death, accidentally sealed in an abandoned fridge in the middle of a rubbish-strewn council estate.

In *Orphans*, four children gather for their mother's wake on the evening before her funeral. During the night that follows they each have a series of misadventures. The oldest, Thomas, insists on staying in the church and maintaining a vigil for the dead mother, as initially does the youngest, his wheelchair-bound and mute sister Sheila. Michael is stabbed in a fight with a young tough who mocks his brothers' open display of grief in a local pub. Rather than seek medical help he aims to exploit his injury by going into work the next day, passing it off as a work-related accident and making an insurance claim. The youngest brother, John, takes it on himself to avenge his brother by tracking down the man who has stabbed him. As the night progresses Sheila leaves the church, becomes stranded when her wheelchair breaks down and is taken in by a family. The church Thomas is sheltering in is partly destroyed by a storm. Michael eventually makes it to work only to collapse on a slipway and be swept out into the docks on a wooden palette. John becomes involved with his disturbed cousin, who provides him with a gun with which to confront his brother's attacker. Eventually, all the family are reunited for the funeral.

One part of *Orphans'* brilliance consists in its movement from the early scenes in the pub, through an increasingly expressionistic use of color, sets and framing. As the night's events spiral into madness, the grief and trauma deepens and the film takes on a tone of harsh Bunuelian surrealism. The one night of *Orphans* represents a symbolic passage through all the forms of civic institution that have been dissolved. The roof is ripped off the church and the funeral ceremony is reduced to an absurd pantomime as Thomas attempts to carry the coffin on his own. Neighbors and the wider community have disappeared, leaving Sheila a mute onlooker on the strife between the family who take her in and their disabled neighbor, while the rancor between classes and desire for revenge embroils John in an attempted rape and the near shooting of a child. Most moving of all is Michael's desperate and ludicrous attempt to parlay the injury he has received from a stabbing the night before into a compensation claim in front of the disbelieving stares of the workmates he enlists as witnesses. By the end all that is left is family, but in *Orphans*, despite its summery coda, the faltering rapprochement between the family members in the cemetery questions whether, in the absence of a parent, fraternity is itself possible.

Family may be the final, fragile bulwark against atomization but that too is not imperishable.

That the orphaning of the central characters is not just the loss of their mother, but the removal of any form of overarching social structure to the lives, is made clear as Michael tries to talk his brother out of pursuing the man who has stabbed him. "Who's going to stop me? There's nobody there". This is the first of two cries up to the sky in *Orphans* (Thomas can only stare up at the sky in awestruck incomprehension as the storm lifts the roof away); the second is Michael's defeated wail, "I want my Mammy!" moments before he collapses in the factory he has struggled all night to reach. This naked, pathetic admission is at the heart of *Orphans'* bravery. It is prepared to figure the neoliberal condition not as a clearing away of the cluttered social terrain so that new adventures can be staged but as an awful trauma, a cosmic disinterment.

*Orphans* has no illusions about what the abandonment of socialism means. Contra the Freidmanite rhetoric, it is exactly neoliberalism with its "structural readjustments" that creates hopeless dependents, that turns adults into children. Reliant on the peregrinations of global capital and the arbitrariness of the market, individuals are divested of any capacity to assert their own interests. Neoliberal maturity is not characterized by the formation of a critique, the deepening of political engagement or a theory of history, but by their asinine and wholehearted rejection. A state of arrested development in which the comfort blankets of "kidult" entertainment, milky nostalgia for the foodstuffs of your childhood, and endless, fretful binges in the toyshop for cool gadgets is the hallmark of the leisure time you work the longest hours in Europe to afford.

## Adam and Paul

Like *Orphans*, Lenny Abraham's *Adam and Paul* (2004) centers on a funeral and takes place over the course of a single day. *Adam and Paul* is a vision of two men in the grip of forces too large for them to understand or control wandering cold, hungry and lost around Dublin trying to find some comfort, whether in the shape of friends, food, money or heroin.

As in *Orphans*, *Adam and Paul*'s series of tragicomic misadventures are caused in some ways by the new interconnections and overlaps brought about by the deregulating, deterritorializing effects of capital itself. There is a kind of negative magical realism at work in both films, wherein the magical elements are experienced as arbitrarily puzzling and horrific. This is the suggestive labyrinthine senselessness of Robbe-Grillet's *Les Gommes*, a novel in which all the normal narrative devices of the detective thriller are collapsed into an endless quest through a cognitively unmappable city, rather than the "transformative" magical realism of *Trainspotting* in which aesthetics and the imagination offer some possibility of escape from the wretchedness of poverty. In this sense both *Orphans* and *Adam and Paul* manage to be about the imagination in a way which does not patronize their central characters.

Intriguingly, both films contain key images that echo *The Wizard of Oz*, itself a Depression-set fantasy of the escape into a more colorful world and a later return to family. The roof is lifted off the church in *Orphans*, whereas in *Adam and Paul*'s opening shot we discover the pair on their back in the middle of a patch of waste ground somewhere on the outskirts of Dublin, Paul mysteriously glued to the mattress he's crashed out on. If Renton leaps into his world, Adam and Paul appear to have been dumped into theirs. It's as though they've been dropped from the sky into an alien world – or had the house they were sheltering in swept away in the night, leaving them stranded and abandoned. In the film's conclusion they will be dumped out on the periphery again, the City, life, the New Ireland, constantly repelling them.

Adam and Paul are singularly useless smackheads: in *Trainspotting*'s terms, they are a couple of Tommys, pathetic and deeply unattractive. There is no heroin-chic here, neither is there any thrilling abjection or outlaw decadence, just sweaty, endless, humiliating need. *Adam and Paul* represents smack-need as a dismal, turgid shamble and beg. Once the smack does fall serendipitously into Adam and Paul's lap the film employs a number of different film stocks, lighting effects and depths of focus to represent the intense illumination of shooting up – an apple core glows hypnotically on a neon bench; Adam and Paul stand gawping in grainy slow motion beneath monolithic tower blocks or in front of gleaming shop fronts.

But smack's merciless logic eventually divides you from everyone else. Adam and Paul are outside all the warm circles that might make life bearable – outside family, outside friendships, the comforts of religion and the rituals of the past. There's a fantasy sequence in which the boys imagine a reunion with the ex-junkie partner, in which the three of them silently, platonically embrace, a fantasy of familial warmth and sensual pleasure. In the process of stealing the TV from the same girl's flat they are distracted by her baby, the rush of sympathetic emotion dulling the pain for a while. But Adam and Paul, unlike Renton, have been permanently exiled. Adam and Paul are useless as rule-bending opportunists and entrepreneurs, and the film effectively casts Tommy as the protagonist of late capitalism. The working class maintain a toe-hold in society through the institutions that remain – the working men's club, the family, the church, a folk tradition that militates against the worst severities of modernization: the son singing tearfully for his dead mother in *Orphans*, the mother singing to forget her dead son in *Adam and Paul*. Those outside are utterly lost. Even Adam and Paul's unit is whittled down to one. The final shot is a dazed Adam discovering his friend has overdosed. He staggers off camera shell-shocked then quickly goes back to search through Paul's pockets for smack.

Neither *Orphans* nor *Adam and Paul* is "feel-good", though both are bleakly comic. In Boyle's films, the sense of the central characters' "journey", so vital to late capitalist product, is one in which the individual achieves some kind of structural adjustment, a refit to reality. The films are a thought experiment for the viewer which reassures them that any alternative to bourgeois consumption was never really going to work after all. They're "feel-good" in the sense that they're therapeutic, realigning characters and audience expectations into identification with reality. But with *Orphans*, there is no central character, no process of nominal destitution and reconstitution, only dispersal and then reconnection: the main character is family itself. No one gets wiser or gets out. In *Adam and Paul* it is impossible to identify who is who (they are always addressed jointly) and the journey only half concludes.

Tellingly, neither film has a commercially viable pop-based soundtrack.

# 3. Everybody Knows This Is Nowhere: *Shallow Grave*

*Shallow Grave*, certainly Hodge's best screenplay, and the first film he and Boyle made together, flaunts its contemporary credentials straight away with a monologue on friends and the sameness of all cities. The attitude toward money in *Shallow Grave* (an attitude found to increasingly less severe degrees in Boyle's work from *Shallow Grave* through to *Millions*) is that money is divisive, if not quite the root of all evil certainly the source of some fairly nasty behavior. It's the love of money that forces the rifts between the flatmates even further apart and leads to the inevitable murderous conclusion. What's interesting in *Shallow Grave* is that finally someone comes out on top, here – Alex, played by Ewan McGregor, managing to outwit both his conniving flatmates and the police. The ultimate moral of the tale is not that love of money will lead on to sure destruction but that you better make sure you're smart and ruthless enough if you want to be rich. Still, there is a residual ambivalence about money and how to get it here that is considerably more muted than in *Trainspotting*, a film which is much more relaxed about people getting filthy rich.

As in *Trainspotting*, the opening monologue tells us a great deal about who the film is addressed to. "If you can't trust your friends who can you trust?" Christopher Ecclestone's corpse inquires of us. "Friends are the new family" was one of the signal phrases of the late eighties and early nineties, reflecting doubtless the (enforced) geographical mobility of the professional classes and the increasing costs of getting a place to yourself. US sitcoms like the immensely popular *Friends* offered utopian, glossy visions of the hilarity and bonhomie of cohabitation while British takes on the theme such as *This Life* and *Game On* (with its memorably agoraphobic couch potato) presented a slightly more wry look at the potential pitfalls.

The friendships in *Shallow Grave* are already ridden with hostilities and competitiveness even before Keith Allen's slick media bullshitter turns up dead in a Caravaggio pose on the bed with a suitcase full of cash underneath it. Indeed, the friends only really seem to enjoy each others' company when they're humiliating unattractive, middle-aged or subcultural would-be flatmates in the film's opening sequence. Irrespective of the fact that the film is setting up the trio as unpleasant types, there is still the invitation to share in the scandalous hilarity of their absurd questions, their pokerfaced delivery, the ironic tone of their dismissals. We're in Loadedland here. The magazine, launched the year before, was aimed at "Men who should know better." This pitch, the guiltless enjoyment of that which is beneath you intellectually/ that which is socially or morally unacceptable on the basis that you know it's wrong and are therefore not fully participating in its wrongness the same way the proles do, is a recurring theme in nineties culture.

But what really snags the attention in *Shallow Grave*'s opening speech is the assertion that the story about to unfold could have happened anywhere. "All cities are the same." This is a bold observation, perhaps even reckless given both how sweeping and dramatically unnecessary it is, the way in which it invites a certain amount of skeptical reflection on the part of the viewer. Are Kinshasa, Oslo, and Jeddah really all the same? What seems most likely, given that the observation is made during a monologue which bemoans the fact that you can't even trust your friends these days is that "cities" is standing in for "people". There is only one type of person now, the middle-class, capitalist subject. Yet the opening sequences show us a variety of people, some of whom are precisely not the required type (it sees that just as some countries are still caught up in History, so some people within the post-Historical world are still caught up in class). Perhaps what is meant, then, is that the conditions of capitalism and the ways in which they deform social relations – both within and between classes – are present everywhere. The film fails to capitalize on this elegiac, intriguing note, relegating it to a flash of zeitgeist cynicism as it busies itself coming on as a Brit equivalent of the Cohen brothers' pastiche-Noir *Blood Simple* (1984).

There is of course another, more immediate, reason why the film feels the need to make this statement early on. Partly it's a plea/apologia for its own mid-Atlantic style, the way it pitches to the States or across the border to England and doesn't want to compromise its chances of a positive reception elsewhere by being too local. This is a determined non-place, reversing the traditional British approach of selling films precisely based on their regional charm/difference.

Much the same applies to the Scotland of *Trainspotting* – or of *Late Night Shopping* (2001) – or the Wales of *Human Traffic* (1999). There no establishing shots of Edinburgh and almost no filming on location. Edinburgh is noticeable by its absence. One shot, anticipating the highly-colored exoticism of *Slumdog Millionaire*, in the sequence just before Renton enters the worst toilet in Scotland, is of a grid of brightly colored windows. The other, when Renton is dragged out into the street by the Mother Superior, contains a distant, gauzy shot of serried ranks of council flats to the strains of "Perfect Day".

By contrast, once Renton moves up to London the first shots of his work and bedsit are presaged by an almost comical number of establishing shots of such a clunkily generic nature that it's hard to determine whether this is in effect a parody, a meta-statement on the tradition of establishing shots themselves, but there is nothing else within *Trainspotting's* vision of London to suggest any kind of playing with representations of the city. For all its attempted irony, it's really the visual equivalent of cheering and flag waving, the film's real emotional identification then is not just with England but with London.

The Scottish are simply some non-Metropolitan other, an exotic tribe of hyperactive rascals whose wit, dynamism and enviable scurrility in fact pales before the firmly grounded central majesty of London. London is where you go for work, to choose life, where you do the drug deals that let you get on the ladder, where life, once again in the form of Keith Allen, is serious. The proles, out in the provinces, may really live, but London is where real people live, London is what matters. Its areas and constituent social types will be anatomized across a number of pictures, not just the fantasy middle-class idylls of *Notting Hill*, but also the hip milieus of Camden in *This Year's Love* (1999) and Brixton in *SW9* (2001) etc. Later still London, as a center of unmappable flows, will be broken up into a series of late capitalist signifiers, (Canary Wharf, The Millennium Dome, Wembley Arena etc). The most notable landmark is Norman Foster's Gherkin, which turns up in everything from *Basic Instinct 2* (2006) to Woody Allen's *Match Point* (2005) to the British made *Straightheads* (2007) and *Outlaws* (2007), all set in an oneiric topographic relation, dislocated New Heritage.

# 4. The English Disease: *28 Days Later, I.D., The Firm, Rise of the Footsoldiers*

## Blessed rage for order

In Boyle and Garland's *28 Days Later* (2002) the problem that has afflicted the population is known as Rage. Passed on from chimps via some well meaning Animal Liberation Front activists, the formerly respectable denizens of the sceptered isle are transformed instantaneously into frothing, homicidal maniacs. A few survive, notably wimpy but nice Jim; Selena, a black female superhero-type complete with *Matrix*-style leather trench coat and a machete; an expendable bullish male; a decent, but expendable, working class dad, and his gutsy and pragmatic daughter, Hannah.

The title tells us: this is how quickly the world can fall apart. *28 Days Later* plays to a number of topical fears: airborne global pandemics, the BSE outbreaks and mass culling of cattle, perennial anxiety over the monstrous secrets buried in the heart of the military-industrial-medical complex, the fearful mobility of Capital itself. In the blink of an eye, swinging London is a ghost town. Busts are always more rapid and unforeseeable than booms. Canary Wharf, from where the project to repopulate Britain will be launched in the superior sequel *28 Weeks Later* (2007), empties out and is abandoned even more quickly than it expanded. If Romero's zombies correspond with the fears generated by an earlier age of Capital, then Boyle and Garland's (along with the more effusive zombies of most mid-nineties-onward zombie movies) express the essence of Hyper-Capital: not the pacified consumer-undead but the ferociously, uncontainably impelled living. Hyper-stimulated, hyper-aggressive, coked up till their eyeballs bleed ...

"Rage" itself is a nineties buzzword par excellence. Road rage, supermarket rage, pavement rage, checkout rage, the word was appended to any facet of modern experience, signifying the instantaneous and uncontrollable irruption of murderous anger over the most minor of disputes and inconveniences. In modern life, tempers fray easily, responses are immediate and intense, the sense of fear over the dangers posed by apparently sanguine fellow citizens is everywhere.

As Jim dies in the original cut of the film, an overly long dream sequence flashes back to the bike accident that put him in hospital in the first place. London is experienced as a city already in the grip of rage, something the disease has potentially only tapped into/accelerated. The disease is the English disease, the stubborn, ineradicable propensity for violence, the simmering tension on the street, in the pub, on the Tube. For Christopher Ecclestone's Major Henry West, people killing people is just business as usual, the rage virus is just daily life, but more so.

A surrogate family of a kind comes together in *28 Days Later* too, though in the original cut of the film it's eventually whittled down to just Selena and Hannah, the men having nobly sacrificed themselves so they can survive. The original ending (it was revised twice, both to offer the certainty of rescue to the survivors and then again so that Jim lives) ties closely in to the themes of Alfonso Cuaron's *Children of Men* (2006) in which the future is with a black women and her baby, the old, white patriarchy having outlived its historical usefulness. In these scenarios a heroic gesture on the part of the central white male is still possible but in the form of a renunciation of his own importance and centrality. There is of course a sneaky, backdoor glorification at work here, since only the martyred white male conscience can guarantee the future, the liberal finding the warrior within in order to destroy or out-maneuver traditional notions of heroic manhood (here the Army) now cast as atavistic and reactionary.

Jim's rage is of the tight-lipped, stoical, pragmatic kind, a coldly impersonal, purposeful murderousness that is not despoiled by jouissance or the directionless stupidity of the mob, thereby allowing him to orchestrate the destruction of a platoon of soldiers. The soldiers are coded as a largely working class rabble, just barely held together by the pretentious upper class Major and then only on the basis that their basest hunger, for women, will be gratified. The worst of the soldiers, the one who takes the most delight in killing the infected and his own disloyal, progressive comrades, who is most forward with the women, keenest to rape, and therefore Jim's nemesis, is the cockney Corporal Mitchell. Having been born within the sound of Bow bells *is the* signifier of unreconstructed, working class masculinity in 90s cinema. In a classic neurotic middle class tradition the upper class in league with the working class threaten the liberal family unit, controlling their destiny through offering protection against the infected, those who, in this Hobbesian accommodation, represent a life outside the citadel that is nasty, brutish and short.

*28 Days Later* acts out the hatred, the destructive desires of the middle classes, through the fantasy of protecting the other supposedly incapable of protecting themselves. The film's final act, set, tellingly, in a requisitioned stately home revolves around the suspense of whether Selena and Helena will be raped by the soldiers before Jim can rescue them.

Again, in this particular film's economy we can see a black women hack up a white man, a father shot in front of his daughter, diseased people repeatedly shot in the head, the population of the country turned against itself, cities deserted or ablaze, but a black woman or a teen being raped by a white soldier is impermissible: this is the horror that the film's climatic tension and release are orchestrated around. What we can see, and are invited even to relish, is Jim putting out Mitchell's eyes with his fingers, symbolizing the breaking of his oedipal relation not just to male authority but specifically to the generalized fear of the animalistic pleasures of the working class male.

Jim's bout of psychopathology is an instrumental affair, a moral obligation divorced from the revelry of the soldiers or the frenzy of the mob. This is killing as it should be, in the name of women and children, no whooping or salivating. A form of "good" rage, purposeful, decent, all the more effective for its moral clarity, is posited as the righteous bequest of the middle classes .The fantasy is the fantasy of a violence without pleasure, ethical violence, liberal violence.

Finally of course it allows for the surrogate family to be brought together again, with Jim able to take on the role of the father/older brother, and Selena becoming the mum now that Hannah has been liberated from a father who was pleasant but unsophisticated and who finally she was wasted on. It is a cross-class, mixed race band who represent the best of England, the future of England. Smart young working class girls destined for university, strong, independent black women, decent men who wouldn't dream of raping anyone and who only access their capacity to kill when it's absolutely necessary.

Intriguingly, in the more subversive *28 Week Later* it is the cowardly and shamed "bad father" who gratuitously and graphically puts out his wife's eyes. The film presents England as a diseased little island whose inhabitants need to be quarantined and left to die. Once you remember that the European Union was originally conceived by Kojeve as a Latin Empire that would stand as a counterbalance to the more virulent strains of capitalism found in the UK and the US, even the most avowed commonsense-peddler would have difficulty not reading the two films in Marxist terms, in which the rage is a particularly accelerated form of Anglo Saxon capitalism, (read, neoliberalism). In *28 Weeks* it is finally necessary to firebomb Canary Wharf in order to eradicate the disease, but it eventually spreads across the channel thanks to the precocious Middle Class kids that Bad Daddy has, regrettably, been unable to kill.

## You mugging me off?

The fantasy of the decent, middle class tough guy, the white-collar university boy as heroic warrior reaches a ludicrous apotheosis in Levi Alexander's *Green Street* (2005). If Guy Ritchie's *Lock, Stock,* (1998) initiates Faux Gangster then *Green Street* initiates Faux Thug. The film's milieu and its mise-en-scène exists in a middle mass of all that is most banal and regressive in BritLand, the Lads' Holy Trinity of sing-a-long Indie, Footie and Booze. The Pub, as a sacred site/ citadel of utopian, homosocial intensities that is initiated by 1999's vastly superior *I.D.* (in which the pub is named "The Rock") is continued through *Green Street* and on into *The Football Factory* (2004). The boys all bond over beer and chasers, having it large and roughhousing to the strains of "Waterfall" by the Stone Roses. In this way at least the film is true both to the way that football-related subcultural groups fused with the emerging E and rave culture in the late eighties, and to the later gentrification of football (all-seater stadiums, colossal price hikes), which coincided with the rise of Indie via New Order's "World in Motion" and Baddiel and Skinner's "Three Lions".

The football firm that teaches Elijah Wood's Matt Buckner how to be a man and finally stand up to his social superiors back in the States via a bizarre, inverted and ersatz class war, is clearly based on the notorious Inter City Firm (ICF), here re-named the Green Street Elite. Charlie Hunnum, who plays top boy Pete, a fresh faced lad straight out of drama school, who has presumably also done some catalog modeling, has the unenviable task of trying to convince the audience that he's the leader of this crew. He's a deeply unconvincing hardman, despite having perfected the shoulders-back, cocky strut from watching Oasis videos, and he isn't helped much by lines of such excruciatingly mixed register that the question of whether the script writer has ever been to England let alone London is constantly in the mind. "You can see where Churchill took a Tom or whatever it is you Yanks do in Jolly Old" "Tom?" "Tom. A tomtit, shit. It's rhyming slang. Like bees and honey for money". "It ain't over yet. Word is these twats are going to have a pop." "They'll be gunning for you too after the job you pulled on their top boy last year."

The phenomenon of the middle class Hooligan first drama-tized in Alan Clarke's *The Firm* (1998) in which the leaders Bex and Yeti are Thatcherite thugs, is taken to absurd lengths in *Green Street*. Every member of the GSE is in a respectable if non-specific profession. Pete is a History and PE teacher, the rest of the boys are summoned from various offices around the capital. The ex-Leader of the Green Street Elite, Pete's brother, Ben "The General" Dunham has abandoned football hooliganism and now lives a life of bourgeois splendor with a glamorous but grounded American, whereas rival Firm, Milwall, personified by stalwart East End villainous cunt Geoff Bell – see also his excellent turn in Nick Love's *The Business* (2005) – are decidedly working class. They eat in greasy cafes, they talk proper Cockney, they look grim and old, have scars and fucked-up teeth, don't wear Stone Island jackets, or, presumably, listen to Cast and Reef. When the call comes through for the Millwall crew leader to mobilize his men he's sitting in the garage in which he works/owns. The last time the two firms met, Bell's twelve-year old son died in a battle, the implication being of course that he is also that most awful of things: A Bad Parent. The film stops short of suggesting that the child's death is a societal blessing-in-disguise but the brief glimpses we are afforded of him are enough to convince the viewer that he was probably going to grow up to be archetypal chavscum anyway.

The concluding battle between the Firms in the wastelands of North Greenwich, played out to some cod-Celtic anthemic rock on the soundtrack, could curl the toes on a prosthetic leg in its attempts to dignify and lionize male aggression as quasi-mystical expression of noble fraternalism. Mel Gibson's *Braveheart* (1995) seems to be at the root of Green Street's climactic battle – and the question of the extent to which *Braveheart* takes its tropes from the hooliganism of the eighties as its model for the gestures of class/national conflict is also worth considering.

Halfway through the final ruck, Shannon, wife to the now hospitalized General and sister to plucky, elfin Matt, mysteriously turns up in a car, for no better reason than that this allows Pete to heroically sacrifice himself so that she and her child might emerge unscathed, deflecting Tommy's anger away from her child and back onto himself by taunting him over the truth that he is ultimately responsible for his son's death by being A Bad Parent. Tommy's rage over the death of his child is seen as disproportionate even by his fellow thugs. He's partly to blame and probably the kid was going to end up just like his dad anyway, unattractive, with bad teeth and a manual job. What's important is that the pretty, sane bourgeois family unit survives, and the middle class boy again heroically sacrifices himself to protect the women and child from the savage, immoderate working class.

The attitude toward the pleasure of drugs that prevails in *Trainspotting* as it does to violence elsewhere in recent British Cinema is, by all means indulge, just don't get carried away. Remember that you have another life. You must not lose face socially, you must not be seen to be overwhelmed or overtaken by anger/pleasure. In *Green Street* as in *28 Days Later,* the working class characters are flawed navigators of the thrill of violence. Mitchell and Tommy Hatcher get carried away and this is their undoing; the overall effect of Tommy beating Pete to death on those watching in *Green Street* seems less horror than embarrassment, whereas both Jim and Pete remain morally clear sighted, open to audience approval, and can still crucially discriminate between right and wrong. There's nothing ontological about middle-class violence.

This is a gentrified hooliganism, an Indie hooliganism where men grow tearful over the lost inclusion in the warm circle of fellow thugs, a bit of fantasy recreational violence "for men who should know better".

## *The aggro eighties*

If there is a certain optimistic, Brit-Film nostalgia for the sixties, for a hyperreal retread of Swinging London as a shiny, techno-savvy, multi-cultural melting pot, a micro-montage of attractions on every street and all the relics of the blighted industrial past converted into homes for the non-laborers of the new economy, as time passes the seventies and eighties re-appear, decades in which a certain amount of non-specific, seemingly apolitical large-scale civil disobedience happened every Saturday, where the Football Hooligans were a thorn in the flesh of the Party of Law and Order. In the revisionist *Away days* (2009), an adaptation of ex-Farm manager Kevin Sampson's novel of the same name, a tenuous link is posited between post-punk acts such as Magazine, Ultravox, and Joy

Division and footie violence. Echo and the Bunnymen are reconstructed in the image of Oasis, and Art School is a lot of pretentious bollocks compared to the authentic, real world pleasures of, as the tagline has it, "Football, Fucking and Rucking".

The British filmmaker this genre is most heavily influenced by is Alan Clarke, who, for all the diversity of his output, is now mostly revered for *Scum* (1997) and *The Firm*. This is largely because they are much more readily assimilated to Lad/style culture than, for example, his powerfully brilliant version of Jim Cartwright's despairing and ferocious anti-Thatcher play *Road* (1987). Clarke's work represents a certain "real" of the pre-Blair years that is now pined for, the irony being that it's precisely only thinkable as a "real" in that it can be made to sit comfortably within the cultural correlates it is presumed to stand against. Significantly, the only use of The Exploited on a soundtrack occurs not in *Trainspotting* but in Clarke's most belligerent vision of the English Disease, *Made in Britain* (1982), the track in question being the David Peace-ishly entitled *UK82*.

Clarke has a reputation as a sober and sobering film maker in a fine British realist tradition. When two of the most successful actors to have worked with him, Tim Roth and Gary Oldman, made their directorial debuts in the UK, it was very much under Clarke's influence. Roth's *The War Zone* (1999) and Oldman's *Nil By Mouth* (1997) both star Ray Winstone in the lead role. *Scum* launched Winstone's career. He disappeared for a decade after 1987 before becoming the Prole-du-Jour in the mid-nineties with the media's shift to celebrating the Authentically British and finding its most heightened expression, handily, right in heart of the capital: that tribe of lovable rogues, Cockneys. Roth and Oldman's films reaffirm a commitment of a kind – or at least, the cynic might suggest, a fashionable desire to demonstrate a commitment – to a type of filmmaking that tackles Social Issues (incest, domestic violence) with unflinching lack of sentimentality. Despite Clarke's reputation for sobriety, in *The Firm*, *Scum* and *Made in Britain*, Clarke's three most memorable meditations on the English Disease, there is a certain punk reveling in the antisocial, the negativity and nihilism of the central characters, a core of intransigently oppositional subjectivity that can neither be co-opted into the comfort of bourgeois living nor broken by the apparatus of State.

In *The Firm*, the English disease is figured as a chronic condition. Bex's murder acts simply as a rallying point for the Firm's to carry on his legacy of expanding into Europe. The Firm are heterotopian, mixed race and mixed class, and in being so present hooliganism as a particularly English condition, stronger than either "race" or class ties, prefiguring the emergence of a postmodern multi-ethnic far-right nationalism oriented around a rhetoric of "Britishness" in the same way that the later *I.D.* (directed by Phil Daniels, who plays Yeti *in The Firm*) anticipates the resurgence of a Far Right element within football itself and Nick Love's *Outlaw* fantasizes a rainbow coalition of cross-class vigilantes standing up for the traditional British Way of Life.


### Shadwell United
On some levels *I.D.* is a simple Jekyll and Hyde Story (a darker variation on the New Man/ New Lad conflict). John has two faces as he tells us at the start, Nice John and Nasty John. Via his involvement with Shadwell Town (here substituting for Millwall) and its fierce pleasures, Nasty John wins out, shattering his respectable bourgeois home life, destroying his belief in his role as a policeman and leading to a spectacularly splenetic moment of confrontation outside his estranged

wife's parents' home. "Here's a promise, when I have kids I'll teach them to hate you. All of you. My kids will fucking come round here and eat yours!"

Hooliganism pre-dates Thatcher but it was in the mid to late eighties that it emerged as public order issue number one (as reflected in *I.D.*) with terrace and city center clashes aiming for maximum social unrest and disruption. It will perhaps be too pat to suggest that this enormous outpouring of negativity and anger, directed ultimately against the State, was quickly pacified by the hippy revivals of House and rave culture, the three consecutive "Summers of Love" effectively defanging a form of protest. Rave was quickly co-opted into the pleasure economy of the nineties via the Superclub and the weekend drug binge. The extent to which E culture acts as a mass-mollifier and a soporific, the ways in which it mutes or channels legitimate angers, the degree to which it was reactionary, will have to be considered elsewhere. Suffice to say this shift is anticipated in *I.D.* Having made Top Boy down hardcore supporters' pub The Rock, John is handed a wrap of coke and invited to join the underworld. The football scene is dying anyway, people will be looking to other pleasures soon, the hardcore hooligan element will be turning to drugs. The lads will be getting luvved up, getting off their tits, having it large. Football can become quietly respectable.

In Nick Love's *The Football Factory* the central problem for lovable weekend hooligan Tommy (the indefatigable Danny Dyer) is boredom, in *The Firm* Bex can't give up the Ruck of a Saturday because he can't live without the Buzz. Once the Buzz can be found elsewhere the violence dies off. *I.D.* suggests that there is a latent political nature to the Firms/hooliganism. John's substitute for the end of his involvement with Shadwell is not the cocaine we see him pour onto his cornflakes, but involvement in Far Right organizations. Perhaps the return of a bland Englishness in the nineties is inconceivable without the neutering effects of a mass uptake of soft drugs. The film's final sequence, with John repeatedly shouting Sieg Heil into the camera with a Union Jack tattoo on his forehead, seeks to draw the obvious parallel between the pleasures of football allegiances and the wider problems of nationalism.

## What's wrong with being happy?

The pub as site of male bonding rituals is central to all the football films. In I.D it's as much the social world of The Rock as the collective euphoria of the matches that seduces the undercover coppers. In one sequence they cut out of a boring dinner with their wives in order to get back there. Nice John's nice life no longer satisfies him. As he begins to fall apart and act in a more contemptuous and bestial way toward his wife she asks him tearfully, "What's wrong with being happy?" As I've already noted, though, there is something more complex going on in *I.D.* than the simple opposition between the pleasant satisfactions of daily life and the ecstatic dimension of match day, though it is certainly a strand in all the Football films, as are the political repercussions of boredom.

The problem of being happy in *I.D* and the nostalgia for the working class community is in some ways a nostalgia for a form of socialization, for a world that has been systematically under attack, first from the Tory governments and then by New Labour. "The Rock" is indicative of geographical fixity, belonging to a particular locale, the laying claim to a territory in the age of deterritorialization (the mantra of all football films is "stand your ground!"). It is also a resistance to the process of gentrification which creates areas in which different economic classes co-exist and the central institutions of life are upgraded or yuppified: gastropubs, wine bars, non-smoking, all-seated. Meanwhile, the working class's set of bizarre rituals and attitudes – from their interpersonal relations to the food they eat, to their leisure pursuits, to their taste in clothes, to the way they talk to their children – has been remorselessly picked over from the middle class perspective on TV and elsewhere in the media.

Rather than the supposition that the working classes stand as a rebuke to the middle classes and that History is with them, now the victorious middle class stand as a corrective to the proles.

But there is a fundamental difference between working and middle class socialization patterns that any notion of classlessness wrongly attempts to elide, condemning one group to submit to an alien regime of value and judgment. Middle class socialization is a form of moral socialization appealing to abstract values, rather than socialization based on positioning within a nexus of family/social relations. The answer to the question "Why" is answered differently: because you're the oldest, a girl, she's your sister, he's from the same street, because I'm your mother, because were poor, as opposed to: because it's not nice, because it's important to share, because every one should take turns.

The first thing John thinks on hearing that "The Rock", that central metaphor for materiality and fixity, is closed is, "no more, Bob. I love you, Bob. No more Gumbo, I love you, Gumbo". The final incomprehension between John and his wife is a consequence of their inhabiting different worlds. In one there is a disembodied subject in a world of objects, in the other an embodied subject in a world of relations. The assumption therefore, that the working class can simply take on a set of middle class values and "be happy", and that their failure to do so is a sign of their belligerence or ineptitude is to posit a fundamental similarity between classes which does not exist. For all its supposed pluralism, Blairite culture casts the working class as inadequate middle class subjects rather than as a different type of subject.

What John gives up in *I.D.* is other people, it's not the football per se that he will miss, his thoughts aren't of Shadwell Town or the Players but of the fellow hooligans, the Rock's regulars.

## Return of the Exploited

"Faux Gangster", a jokey, capering, ironic take on the under-world that was started by *Lock, Stock* and *Love, Honour and Obey* (2000) and was continued by Nick Love's heavily *Trainspotting*- and *Fight Club*-influenced *Football Factory* has matured over the past few years, becoming considerably more interested in recent British social history. Nick Love's work is still overly indebted to the Journey motif and the feel-good resolution and in this respect he's too close to other Blairite filmmakers like Boyle and Ritchie, though his most recent film (a remake of Clarke's *The Firm* is pending) *Outlaw* is an attempt to imagine a mixed race/class troop of Travis Bickles stepping in where the Law has failed and has the singular distinction of being the only film known to this writer in which Tony Blair is called "a cunt". Love's avowed aim in *Football Factory* was to dispel the myth of a classless Britain, but his view of class is intertwined with the rhetoric of Values and notions of Britishness. Nonetheless Love is a genuinely popular filmmaker who is interested in pressing questions about the state of British society and is addressing them through an engaging pulp form.

While the quality of the Hooligan films is variable, they have the distinction of being genuinely home-grown, grassroots successes. Not only this, but they have bred a troop of key character actors who revolve between directors, giving them something of the charm of studio movies of old. *Essex Boys* (2000) and *Rise of the Footsoldiers* (2007) represent the intelligent end of the genre. Both films revisit the Rettendon Range Rover murders of 1995, a gangland execution in Essex, speculating on the back-story. Julian Gilbey, who made the underwhelming

*Rolling with the Nines* before considerably upping his game with *Footsoldiers*, is that rare thing in British genre cinema, a highly technically competent director, editor and writer. There are plenty of the standard hard-cunt voiceover tropes, especially in *Rise*, and a certain clumsily expository quality to the dialogue, but these occasional shortcomings are more than compensated for by the visual intelligence, and the use of English scenery and cityscapes in both films. *Essex Boys* in particular manages to make Britain's wintry grayness and concrete aesthetically compelling and benefits from a tough female protagonist. *Rise of the Foot Soldiers* is more self-consciously in debt to Scorsese's *Goodfellas* (1990), as *Essex Boys* is in debt to John Dahl's Noir-retread *The Last Seduction* (1994), but the action is handled with real aplomb, mapping the trajectory of career criminal Carlton Leach (Ricci Hartnett, Cillian Murphy's nemesis in *28 Days*) through the Thatcher and Major years, tracing the continuum from football violence to rave culture to organized crime hinted at in *I.D.*.

Something of the scouring negativity of Clarke's films is partially returned to here. *Footsoldiers* is extremely keen to distance itself from any political claims at the start: "You know what, we weren't trying to change the world; we were just looking for a fucking tear up." "We were all over the papers the next day, going on about how we was the biggest menace since the IRA, but what the fuck did we care? We was just having a laugh".

But in showing the state of permanent fear in which Leach now lives, (the final freeze-frame is on Leach's grim, weary face as he leaves another hideout) something of the central conflict within the working class Thatcherite, for whom the term "Essex boy" will always be a metonym, is revealed: the desire for radical change, for the release of pent-up energies, on the one hand, and the catastrophic effect of what you have brought down upon yourself on the other.

The use of real events and characters intermixed with speculation, stock and filmed footage means that *Footsoldiers* also overlaps in some ways with Stephen Frears' *The Queen* (2006) as does Jon Baird's extremely worthwhile contribution to the Hooligan genre, *Cass* (2008).

*Cass* is much more directly politically engaged than Baird's earlier short film, *It's a Casual Life* (2003), which is wearyingly obsessed with the nuances of East London speech and style, and predictably insists on reassuring the viewer that there was absolutely no political unconscious at work in eighties hooliganism. (A part of this determination again derives from Clarke's *The Firm* in which the members of the crew mock a TV sociologist's pronouncements on their motivation.) *Cass* is closely based on the writings of someone who actually lived through the seventies and eighties rather than a twenty-something's "re-imagining" of them. The central character is a black football hooligan and later nightclub bouncer who became notorious in the eighties as the leader of the Inter City Firm. The film pays quite a lot of attention to Thatcher, along with class and race, as determinants in hooliganism. For Cass, violence is an essential component of Englishness. "We're a warring nation. We're born to fight", he tells a TV interviewer.

There is a rage that is fundamental to English life that no amount of postmodern glossing can cover. *Rise of the Footsoldiers'* first monologue begins strikingly: "It was the end of an era, but before the murders, the tortures, the beatings and the Ecstasy, before all of that there was football. You see, football was where the spite and the hatred first came from."

The question is where that spite might take us next. Will there be an extension of the nexus of sport, criminality and the Far Right as prefigured in *I.D.* and already beginning to take shape with the English Defence League, or merely further orgies of Gangster excess? Most importantly, can it be recuperated to any progressive political ends at all?

# Intermission: A note on Sunshine

Danny Boyle's *Sunshine* (2007), scripted by Alex Garland, certainly appears to be the director's biggest budgeted work to date. A team of scientists attempt to reignite the sun, which in its dwindling has buried the earth under a layer of permafrost. The multinational cast, representing the cream, one supposes, of international co-operation, are eventually, through mishaps and foul play, reduced to Cillian Murphy. The film, rather like Paul Anderson's initially promising *Event Horizon*, which its second act rips off, doesn't know where to go with its premise, and ends up deciding that what audiences pine for is Freddy Kruger in Space. The monster here is again one of the bogeymen of the late capitalist Id, the fanatic, the man who has stared into the sun, the man who has thought too much, questioned too deeply, enjoyed to too great a degree, and who has decided the world doesn't need saving. If the soldiers in *28 Days Later* are too bestial, then Pinbaker is too refined, a Fundamentalist. The world is self-evidently worth saving, and save it Cillian does, again by sacrificing himself so that humanity may live. The final scenes reveal to us the humanity that all this titanic interstellar effort has gone into saving: poor huddled masses, the elderly shivering in wretched homes, gangs of impoverished teenage boys? No: it's a nicely dressed young middle class woman and her kiddies in a snowy park that are chosen to represent the future humanity it's all been done in the name of. Perhaps we can assume that by the time the sun burns out in the sky we actually will "all be middle class now".

# 5. All Saints:
## *Millions*

*One man, with a dollar in the right place, can change the world*

Boyle's *Millions* (2004) is a neoliberal propaganda piece par excellence and, handily, it is also a children's film – if such a thing can be said to exist anymore in our brave new world of Kidultinfotainment.

A child discovers a bag full of money, he and his brother argue over what to do with it. The younger, more spiritually inclined child sees incarnations of Christian saints all around him, but unlike those abnormal children who have short attention spans, rebel against authority and need tranquilizing, *this* child has special abilities rather than special needs. He wants to give it away to help the needy, while his older brother (representing, at the age of twelve, no doubt the value system of an older, more cynical age, before Caring Capitalism spread its balm over us all), wants to reinvest it in property, use it to widen the sphere of his influence and basically get more muff behind the bike sheds. First you get the money, as Tony Montana well knew.

Written by ostensible lefty Frank Cottrell Boyce, *Millions* is a critique of materialism on only the most superficial level. The brothers live in a picturesque new suburban development, portrayed as an enchanted space: we see the wonders of the construction industry at work in a rapid CGI simulated housebuild in which, naturally, no actual laborers are present. This is how houses come about in the post-Industrial economy, magicking themselves into being and then indefinitely gaining in value. The family has gone up in the world, leaving the streets of terraced houses behind, and the father is in the booming building trade himself. We're all middle class now and forever; there is no spectacular housing bubble waiting to burst and any idea that the worst financial crash of all time is looming beyond the pleasant green hills is simply alarmist scaremongering.

But just because England is a demi-paradise and want has been banished from our shores, that doesn't mean that we, on an individual level, of course, don't have a responsibility. Not at all: we have a Faith School-friendly, Roman Catholic-converting Blairite Holy responsibility to heal the sick and suture closed [ the wounded places of the earth. The film is there to proselytize to us about the necessity of charity in what used to be called the Third World, until it was rebranded as the Developing World, so people could feel that they were heading in the right direction and not stuck anywhere indefinitely. England does have a couple of friendly, healthy-looking, young kids selling the Big Issue who are whisked off to Pizza Hut for a slap up feast. They are suitably grateful, the deserving poor always are, but not really poor enough, being English, to really need any of the boys' money. Pizza Hut is just one of the many Caring Capitalist Corporations that crowd *Millions'* mise-en-scène. Those other paradigms of corporate responsibility Coke, Pepsi, and Nike are also semi-permanently on display, targeting the spongy, virginal brains of the kiddies watching, in the hope that, after the film has been seen, the nag factor will boost the demand for soft drinks, trainers and stuffed crusts in the multiplex park's usefully identikit set of retail opportunities. A part of the problem for the older brother is his inability to wed capitalism to a divine sense of responsibility. As in *Trainspotting*, like *Shallow Grave*, the money that is left to the children to disburse appears from nowhere, initially seeming to have been conjured out of thin air by the same weightless economic means that constructs houses. Actually it's been stolen, but isn't the important thing about money that no matter how you get hold of it you give a little back, observing a minimal piety which will safeguard your soul and ward off any potentially pleasure-disrupting feelings of guilt?

There is also an identification in *Millions* of women with a compassionate capitalism, foreshadowing the claim of New Labour's Minister for Women and Equality, Harriet Harman, that the recent financial crisis would have been avoided if women had been in charge. The well-fed Daisy Donovan is collecting for "poor children", the children's late mother (who appears as a saintly apparition toward the end of the film) assures him that his brother has a good heart, he just needs a little help to see what's really important, i.e. not a life of high material comfort, the one Renton set out to enjoy, but a life in which it is understood that giving is also a form of pleasure. Doing good and consumer pleasure need not be mutually exclusive: this idea was of course trailblazed around the time by Bono's Red credit card and his "punk capitalism", sold to us in at least one memorable ad by the image of a woman bifurcated down the middle: on one side she is white and western, laughing with shopping bag in hand, perhaps knowing that she is about to meet her attractive but responsible and caring banker husband to enjoy a cocktail or two in an exclusive bar, on the other she is an African tribeswomen carrying a spear and leaping for joy, perhaps knowing that now due to the white woman's selflessly spending on her Red card her children won't die before their first birthday. How to get them to their second? Why, just keep shopping!

The only black faces seen in the film are those of a smiling and grateful Other located on the far side of the world and certainly not an aggrieved and harassed ethnic minority at home, but then Boyle's England is as remorselessly white as Richard Curtis'. In the final sequence – again drawing on the *Wizard of Oz,* so weirdly entrenched in late capitalist Id – the play house magically whirls the family away to Africa where a group of grinning Nigerians splash water over themselves and their visitors in a celebration of the munificence of the caring souls in the West who have given them the gift of life. Most importantly, in the final freeze frame of the boy's smiling face, the message that helping others need not be anything other than fun is memorialized: enjoyment and privilege are guaranteed to remain the right, all that's needed is a little disbursement, the life of the poor depends upon the compassion of the wealthy countries and they are our grateful dependents.

God bless the child that's got his own.

# 6. Between the two deaths:
## *The Queen*

Queen: (amending speech) "What I say to you now I say to you from my heart and as a grandmother."
Jarvin: "Do you think you can say it?"
Queen: "Do I have a choice?"

Stephen Frears' complex, mordant *The Queen* (2006) is a view of the Blairite project to "modernize" Britain as seen from the perspective of one household, the house of Windsor.

It's a film which has perhaps been overlooked, not featuring in any recent Best British Films polls. Yet it is certainly an audacious work, one that only someone of Frears' experience and, possibly reckless, confidence would even attempt. A film which does so much that feels original and sidesteps so many genre pigeonholes that it requires and rewards multiple viewings.

*The Queen* quickly establishes a spilt in the orders of representation. The first shots are grainily pixelated TV footage of the eve of Tony Blair's election – there are jubilant faces, applauding hands, and quickly Blair himself, played by Michael Sheen (an actor as central to post-Cool Britannia British Cinema as Ewan McGregor was to nineties BritFilm) being interviewed by a reporter. We move from this to the Queen (Helen Mirren) watching the events on a portable TV while having her portrait painted and discussing the recent election. The title sequence is a shot of Mirren, static in her chair in full regalia, against a black backdrop. To an orchestral score, the camera moves up her body, transforming her into a living monument that turns unexpectedly toward the viewer in the final seconds of the shot, gazing enigmatically out of the frame as the film's title comes up on the screen beside her. Blair is TV, hot, clammy, close-up; the Queen is portraiture, sculpture, film.

The battle that's played out in the Queen is coded on several different levels. It is at once the battle of the mediascape against privacy, of the new establishment against the old, of the Celebtocracy against the Aristocracy (itself a restaging and continuation of the battles of the emerging sixties against the declining fifties), of TV against all other forms of media, of the fanatsmatic classless mass against the last bastion of a consciously classed elite, of sobriety against hysteria, of reserve against emotionalism. The film formalizes these struggles through a complex diegetic tension between real and staged TV footage and filmed versions of real events. The only "real" people in the film are Diana (though she is also glimpsed in a brief restaged moment entering her car as it sets off through Paris and is pursued by paparazzi) along with her brother Earl Spencer. Documentary footage is made to inhabit the same fictional space as the Royals and the Blairs. An inevitable and conscious dissonance is created by the choice to not simply restage everything and by the choice of actors. No-one here bears any especial resemblance to the people they play; there is none of the traditional biopic fastidiousness of finding "lookalikes": the mimetic is a second order consideration in *The Queen*, as is spectacle. The film is neither biopic, nor Heritage cinema. It is instead fundamentally concerned with representation, its role in ideology and power.

The collision between Blair and the Queen is the collision on one level of hot and cold media, and on another and related level of the messianic and the divine. The Queen's seeming intractability on returning to London is explained by her advisor Jarvin as a consequence of her believing that "it's God's will she is who she is", a belief echoed back to her by the Queen Mother as they stroll in the garden at Balmoral. The divine is auratic and silent, it commands; the messianic is charismatic and discursive, it persuades. On their first meeting Blair and Cherie are advised on the protocol to follow when they enter "the presence" (this is what the Queen is described as – an abstracted, otherworldly entity). Cherie, ever the smirking Republican, questions the term. Blair insists on being on first name terms with everyone, much to the Queen's distaste. Tony may have charm, may have "people skills" but he is not a Presence. On kissing the Queen's hand, accepting his role as her Prime Minister, she visibly breaks away from his touch. It's an ambiguous moment. Perhaps his lips have burned her.

## Blair

It's made explicit early in the film that Blair has an Establishment background, much more so in fact than either of his Tory predecessors – he had the same Tutor as The Prince of Wales ("well, we won't hold that against him", joshes the Sovereign) – and that he has also promised the greatest constitutional reform for a century. The unlikelihood of any attacks on inherited wealth and privilege, of any substantial dismantling of the class system actually happening, is immediately underlined by the first shots of Blair drawing up outside Buckingham palace star-struck and reverent.

There are also two key moments in which Blair is preparing early speeches. He is interrupted by one of his advisors who feels he should be appending the word "Labour" to Prime Minister, Blair waves the term a way as an irrelevance. Later coming across the word "revolution" in a different speech Blair panics. "Who wrote this stuff?" he asks in dismay. His aides are nonplussed. Massive constitutional reform is expected, he has been given a huge mandate by the British people, his aides explain to him. The camera holds on his shocked expression, the realization that he really is expected to make significant changes to the order of things.

In *The Queen* Blair effectively rescues the monarchy, forcing it to adopt a form of classlessness, to bow to public pressure and undercut class with the acknowledgement of sentiment, "showing us there is a heart in the House of Windsor". The amendments made to the Queen's speech by Blair's notorious spin doctor, Alastair Campbell, focusing on her desire to protect and comfort the boys and expressing her admiration for Diana, make the Queen occupy the position, not of a monarch but of grandmother, speaking not from her Palace but from her heart, not a sovereign addressing her subjects, but also just a grandmother looking at the people and asking them to love her. She participates in the classless universalism of what-we-all-are-inside. Everybody says "I Love You". Everybody hurts.

In this way the monarchy's perpetuation is ensured. Classlessness is understood as an attitude, a form of self-presentation. The inside of Number Ten Downing Street is a clutter of books and knick knacks, guitars and overflowing papers. Blair insists that his retinue call him Tony. Classlessness is purely performative. It does not consist in the abolition of Eton and Oxford but in not talking as though one has gone to them. Classlessness is about no longer caring about the old signifiers of class, or the old character traits, it's not about any structural changes, as Blair's face at the mention of the word "revolution" makes clear. If class doesn't make any real difference to how we behave any more, then maybe it doesn't exist. More smoke and mirrors.

The divine derives its legitimacy from the ultimate authority, this is the cause of its solidity and silence, its imperturbable calm – it needs no justification, it's ontologically resolved; the charismatic has only its own performance as legitimating agent, hence its frantic evanescence, its neurotic need to constantly check its performance against opinion polls and column inches, the hysteria that this perpetual watchfulness inculcates. Painting and sculpture, the two forms with which the Queen is identified at the start of the film, are not media in flux, they represent a wholeness and a fixity, whereas TV, the media of Blair and Diana, with its endless succession of conflicting attitudes, reports, polls and opinions, continuously undermines any prospect a of settled and stable self.

These are also in some ways the distinctions between atavistic elites (the Royals and their retinue) and a "modern" classless middle mass: between epochs.

Repressed and mounting hysteria run throughout the film, and this is not just the hysteria of the growing crowds. From the start there is an implication that the mood in the country is feverish. The response to Diana's death was perhaps a further efflorescence of the massive psychic relief that followed from the Tories finally being defeated after their seemingly impossible re-election in 1992, raising the question of whether Diana dying a few months later or earlier may have garnered a much more muted response. "There is a growing sense of excitement," an announcer tells us as the Queen watches the election-day events unfold on her portable TV. Blair is also a hysterical figure. In his address directly after Diana's death he uses the term "People's Princess", his voice breaking. The newsreader struggles to contain his emotion as a result. The women of the Queen's household clustered around the television weep. Blair hysterisizes the population, then forces the Royals to adapt to them in order to realign expectations about any changes he might make. In saving the monarchy he temporarily saves himself.

"The People's Princess". In *The Queen* these words act as a kind of contagion, cooked up by Campbell with Blair's quavering voice and hand wringing earnestness the delivery system. He does not capture the mood of the nation but induces it. Campbell is portrayed as a ruthless sentimentalist, coining the term "people's princess" only an hour after the accident, amending the Queen's speech so it seems "more like it came from a human being". But, in the film, all the humanity is with the Royals – humanity understood here as restraint, decorum, dignity. Campbell by contrast is an inhuman figure, compulsive and sneering, a brilliant manipulator of emotions yet apparently without any himself. Campbell is frigid, Blair a hysteric, only the Royals have the temperament for grief and loss.

## Diana

Diana, the film's absent center, is represented by a montage of TV newscasts and photographs, including retreads of the interview in which she begged for public approval. There is something new emerging in *The Queen*. This new world, of which Diana is the "Queen of Hearts", is one in which republican sentiment is replaced by a republic of sentimentality. What almost brings the Queen down is not the obscenity of her profligate wealth, but her refusal to express emotion, to become a mere celebrity, to submit to the democratic impulse toward the state of post-historic absolution in which one's structural role is eclipsed by the familial and interpersonal. The Queen has moved from the frozen, enigmatic realm of iconography into the world of TV. In the sequence where the Queen delivers the speech, she is seen both as a TV and film image; she has taken on a kind of doubleness, a minimal coloration from the world of the charismatic. Soon she will be

"Her Maj" and, unimaginably, Brian May will be playing on the roof of Buckingham Palace for her Jubilee.

There are two looks to camera in the Queen. The first is that given by the Queen herself in the title sequence, a moment of wry, chilly appraisal. The second follows Earl Spencer's funeral speech, an attack on his sister's treatment by the royals in which he praises her as "genuinely classless". The Queen fidgets in discomfort and the film cuts to a slow motion shot of Diana looking up toward the camera. The look goes both into the film, it's a look at the Queen herself, and out through the fourth wall simultaneously, positioning both the Royals and the viewer in an alignment. Here, Diana occupies a kind of extra-diegetic space, some third place that collapses the film and the audience onto the same plane, creating a continuum of spectatorship that traverses the screen itself. This moment brilliantly and uniquely symbolizes the shift of the relationship between the Royals and the people, the ways in which Diana's death has forced the Royals to occupy the same space and position in relation to her as the people occupy. (A few scenes earlier, the Queen has gone freely among her subjects for the first time since Armistice day, we are told.) It asserts the supremacy of Celebrity, of the New Classless England in which we are all subjects before the power of TV.

## The TV

TV is everywhere in the Queen, a mysterious almost divine entity in its own right. It's to oracular TV that both the Royals and the Government itself must turn in order to understand what is happening, what's being asked of them; it's TV that guides them toward what they must do. TV invades the security of Balmoral, bringing back the specters of the dead, pictures of the inexplicable discontent building at the palace gates, the Gnostic voice of the people.

TV is also slyly used in the conversation between Cherie and Tony Blair, echoing their mindsets. Tracy Ullman is busily pontificating on CNN about fifteen years of Establishment Tory rule and the wonderful young Prime Minister Tony Blair and how Britain is begging for change. Cherie's interest is piqued, something is happening here, something potentially revolutionary and Republican. She chimes in with what is being said on the TV. Blair is defensive, claiming no one wants the monarchy abolished: the TV chimes in with him. More quickly than would be possible in the real time of the film, Ullman's interview is over and the Constitutional historian and deep conservative David Starkey is now being interviewed. There's a flash of stock footage in which Starkey says "the queen cannot change" and then back to Blair. It's an intriguing momentary rupture in the film's realism, a flash of Blair's hidden nature; there's an implication for a second that TV is a liquid medium on which the consciousness of the bickering couple is acted out by others. You respond to the TV and it responds to you, it will always tell you what you want to hear. TV is consciousness itself.

### The stag

It's tempting to read the stag that The Queen suddenly encounters as she stands sobbing by the lake as representing Diana. Her response on seeing it – "Oh. You're a beauty" – suggests a rapprochement of a kind with Diana, an acknowledgement of her "amazing" qualities, but that is not in keeping with the rest of the film. The stag stands for the monarchy itself. The Queen chases it away from the hunting party comprised of Prince Philip and the boys. Philip is the voice of reaction, or sanity, depending on where one is positioned in relation to events, and it is he who is most likely to destroy the monarchy. By chasing it out of Philip's clutches she wins a momentary reprieve.

But this is not the last of the stag. As the Royals leave Balmoral, Philip announces that the stag has been shot on a neighbor's estate, a private estate. The Queen goes over to see it and discovers the animal hanging from its feet, head removed in an outhouse: a potent symbol of her fears about the potentially insurrectionary mood in the country.

It has been shot by a banker. Here we see the porous barrier between the worlds of old and new money, the danger posed by the newly hyper-rich, hyper-confident classes of financiers and celebrities, money men down from London. They are poor shots and their incompetence, while it is to be deplored, only causes the animal greater suffering in the end.

## The corgis

Something of Frears' artistry can be seen in the scene by the lake, the boys out of focus in the background as the Royals discuss the mounting hysteria back in London and the calls to display the flag above Buckingham palace at half mast. The Queen is wavering, more affected by the news seeping into her solitude every day via the television screen than her husband who is blithely indifferent to public opinion. As the Queen enters the scene, she's followed by her corgis, who take up residence out of shot. As the conversation progresses they form a kind of chorus, the Queen throwing some scraps of food to them as they watch and wait. Philip assures her that the situation will blow over in a couple of days, the Queen appears unconvinced. The next shot is archive footage of the queues to sign Diana's memorial book that proves Philip has been over-optimistic. In the final frames of the scene by the lake the corgis run in from off screen and begin to caper around the royal feet, a sudden invasion of the frame, a flurry of activity upsetting the neatly composed shot. At the end of the film as Blair and the Queen stroll chummily through the palace grounds, the corgis are back again bouncing merrily along beside them.

## The boys

In an act of great restraint Diana's two children are kept off camera or at least in the background throughout the film. There is no attempt at cheap emotional gratification in the film by focusing on their pain. A staunch Republican like Frears can still mourn the passing for a certain type of Englishness as embodied by the Royals without wishing for the monarchy to continue. He can still be saddened by the sober, stoical, detached, controlled element of Englishness gradually yielding under the pressure of compulsive confessionalism and opinionism.

## Charles

Charles is much more anxious to "modernize" than the old guard. He willingly submits, while the Queen is forced to. It is significant that his moment of greatest humiliation and therefore greatest increase in popularity is his re-enactment of the excruciating and pivotal scene in the dole office from *The Full Monty* (1997) in which the ritual of signing on is transformed into a magically comedic moment by hip-swiveling and thrusting along to Donna Summer: you may be on the scrapheap for life now but don't worry, if you find your creativity and express yourself it will all be so much easier. This substitution of the monarchy desperate to legitimate itself for the proles desperate to find some way out is a symbol of the dominance of the middle class, as was the message on his fiftieth birthday cake: "The Full Monarchy".

## The second death

The other significant death in recent British popular culture is that of Jade Goody, which happened in 2009, twelve years after Diana's death.

A former Big brother contestant, her lack of formal education and politesse, weight problems and interpersonal conflicts maintained her prominence in the tabloids and celebrity magazine throughout the noughties. The pleasure of *Trainspotting* or *The Full Monty* in part derives from watching the chavscum lay their own lives to waste. This is of course accompanied by a concomitant sentimental disavowal, a tendency that reached its apex with the perverse interrelation between the deaths of Diana and Jade Goody. Goody's protracted demise from cancer in the media represented a genuinely obscene reveling in the humiliating minutiae of the death of the representative chav hate-figure disguised as a compassionate involvement, a narrative of a young mother's death orchestrated to reach its apotheosis in a wave of redemptive sympathy. The proles redeem themselves through dying well, stoically and humbly; but while they live, their vulgarity is an offense to middle class good taste. Again there is a compact between the classless aristocrat, Diana, and the risen chav, one in which the movement is toward the middle. The Aristocracy needs to be less reserved, aloof, obsessed with decorum. It redeems itself by becoming more proletarian: with Goody it's the opposite movement, the proles redeem themselves through dying well, stoically and with forbearance, taking on the characteristics of the higher orders. The proles may dance and sing but finally this isn't servility enough, they must die well and be seen to do so to truly become classless at last. This is how Jade passes from being The Pig, as she was dubbed in her early Big Brother days by The Sun, to being lionized as A Saint, not just by offering up her pain for consumption, but by offering up her death.

# 7. X Factors:
## *Slumdog Millionaire, Mama Mia*

Boyle's *Slumdog Millionaire*, we are told, is a feel-good movie par-excellence, as is Phyllida Lloyd's *Mama Mia*. The films were British cinema's two major successes in 2008. *Slumdog Millionaire* is a British film in that as it was scripted and directed by Brits and its success at the Oscars was widely seen as a triumph for the indigenous film industry: it provided the most significant Oscar triumph since Collin Welland and Hugh Hudson's considerably more sober *Chariots of Fire*, while *Mama Mia* is the highest grossing film at the British box office ever.

But in what does *Slumdog*'s "feel-good factor" reside? Perhaps it is simply the enduring pleasure of seeing a decent guy battle against adversity to find love, a rags to riches story of human fortitude and endeavor, but this is to overlook what's odd about *Slumdog Millionaire* in terms of traditional heroic narratives. The reconciliatory element of many of Boyle's films rests in the traversal of an oppositional position, as in *The Beach* or *Trainspotting*. There is a minimally active subject in both films, the heroes are presented as consciously aware of their own condition (via voice over) and decision-making to a degree, negotiators of a system that is relatively open, or at least open to them, in which they are positioned in such a way that there is always the option to "choose life". Whatever critical positions may be taken up on this type of representation are largely irrelevant here, the shift from the sense of an active (white, western) subject to the almost entirely passive central hero of *Slumdog Millionaire* is what catches the attention. If we take *Trainspotting* at face value and assume that what allows Renton to complete his "journey" is his intellect and resourcefulness, then Jamal in *Slumdog Millionaire* is a pure accident of his own experience; he's non-self-directing, getting to his own narrative resolution through purely autotelic means. This is not even the idea that "character is destiny", simply that there is destiny. Jamal knows all the answers in Slumdog not due to any concerted effort on his part but due to some ineffable fit between his personal history and the requirements of the show.

It's partly this that appeals so deeply to the British viewer circa 2008. A vision of a universe in which salvation equals escape, in the form of money and true love. Success derives not from any special talent or fortitude (the minimal moral gratification provided by the old myths) but simply through an ineluctable compact between experience and the world's requirements. In using the term "world" here we may as well use the term "market" or even "media", the situation by this stage is that the media has taken on a transcendent role in the culture, especially in British culture: the media is now a benevolent deity conferring riches and status, through quiz or talent shows, the liberation-through-entertainment of *The Full Monty* and *Billy Elliot* (2000) are now entrenched in the lifeworlds of the population (it's surely no coincidence that *Slumdog Millionaire* is adapted by Simon Beaufoy, the writer of *The Full Monty*). The important thing is getting out and one does so by "performing", or in the case of Big Brother's even more radical de-existensializing of the subject, by simply *being*. Forget agency, get yourself an Agent. What one has, above and beyond talent, above and beyond personality, is an intangible additional element, an X factor that confers success among a group of minimally-different products and personae, something that precisely correlates with the market's invisible hand, partially materialized for the advertisements for England's fledgling National Lottery along with the slogan "it might be you". Choose your numbers and keep your fingers crossed, sing your song and grit your teeth, *just be* and perhaps you will be rewarded, swept up out of your poverty in the final frame, in the closing seconds, by the hand of destiny, the voice of the public, the deus ex media.

The response to desperate precarity, to a universe on which one has no purchase, is a return to faith. Not everyone can prosper but the god is essentially benign. Everyone joins in celebrating Jamal's success, the poor throng to the windows of electrical goods' stores to watch the TVs they will never be able to afford, celebrating that one of their kind has been elected. Why is he one step away from winning a million rupees? the film asks us at the start, offering up a number of options. The correct answer is of course "D" – "It is written". He hasn't cheated, he's too good for that. He wasn't lucky, even bad people can get lucky. He certainly isn't a genius. That would be deeply uncongenial to any fantasy that a similar destiny may await us too.

What also allows Jamal to succeed, the reason he is the gods' favorite, is his purity. A part of *Slumdog's* popularity is its Victorianism: it's hard not to read Boyle's India as a fantasy projection of England, a Dickensian world of fixed hierarchies and chaste and pure hearted beggar children who fall in with a bad crowd and are eventually rescued by benign patrons, where the police indulge in a bit of knockabout electrocution and torture, where no-one's life is ultimately ruined by their travails, where decency prevails, where the dynamic energy of capitalism is a source of dizzying wonder. *Slumdog* might be a re-imagining of *Oliver Twist* in which the role of the kindly patron, the good bourgeois who recognizes and rewards purity of heart, is taken on by the mediascape itself.

Our heroes in *Slumdog Millionaire* are, of course, Orphans, the figure of the orphan being one of the great sentimental icons of paternalist capitalism. If only England were like this! Which is not to suggest, of course, that England isn't.

The Nairn-Anderson thesis recasts class as caste: the "glorious thirty years" of the post-war period is a brief, fantastic interregnum in the deep-time of the English caste system, the classlessness of the Blair years an entirely fantasmatic glossing of the slow re-sedimentation of a momentarily shaken social order. *Slumdog Millionaire* represents a part of the re-establishing of hierarchy in England in which the authority of the Aristocracy, of divine right is re-established, re-divinized as the rule of the media. If *The Queen* dramatizes the clash between media, between TV as the always on, dynamic, hyper-real flow of info-capital and the settled world of portraiture and film, then in *Slumdog Millionaire* TV has assumed the place of the Divine, it is the agency through which God expresses His will.

Jamal escapes his poverty, though this is not his aim. He is too pure for that, he merely wants to be re-united with his true love, but handily the corollary of his appearance is enough cash to make sure that Latika can be kept in the new Mumbai style to which she has not merely become accustomed but looks to have been born to. Here is another way in which *Slumdog Millionaire* overlaps with the tradition of the English novel and again with *Oliver Twist*. The money that Jamal wins was always-already his, for it is written, rather as Oliver is the child of the bourgeoisie and was always only holidaying in poverty, one must be innocent of money to truly deserve it. *Trainspotting* tries to tantalize us with the freedom of poverty, *Millions* grows Pious and exhorts us to do something about it via charity, but *Slumdog Millionaire* tells us to relax, there is another mechanism, one which shapes all our ends. In all three films our heroes receive money for and from nothing.

*Slumdog's* quiz show money is the purest of course, the revenue generated from advertising products and services that somewhere down the line have people bashing phones as Jamal does, or mining ore, or sewing garments seem so remote from the magical world of the quiz show, from the protective, enchanted dome of the *Millionaire* arena.

*Slumdog Millionaire* bears a more that passing resemblance to *Trainspotting*, and not just in its laborious overuse of the chase. The boys in *Slumdog Millionaire* are even luckier than Renton. They get to start having their adventures in capitalism almost as soon as they can walk, and while we can't even see Renton trawl his arm through any convincing looking shit in *Trainspotting*, we can happily see a little Indian boy immerse himself in a lake of it and emerge covered head to toe. In fact this is a broadly comic moment in the film, compared to *Trainspotting's* attempt at gross-out. There's something revealed here about identification. Jamal's trials and suffering are essentially a delight, we wince with Renton as we imagine ourselves in his situation, but Jamal is just a cheeky little brown boy and for him swimming through shit is merely more of the crazy fun that slum kids enjoy on a daily basis. The fact that Jamal is prepared to swim through shit to get a star's autograph while Renton only has to fish through a toilet to get his suppositories says something about the power of celebrity, the way in which the sick and infirm flock to the Star as they once flocked to be touched by the king.

The major influence behind both *Slumdog Millionaire* and *Mama Mia* is Bollywood. Both these films' use of Bollywood tropes suffers by comparison with the work of Mira Nair. In Nair's excellent adaptation of Thackeray's *Vanity Fair*, Bollywood acts as a corrective to the effacement of colonialism in the closed bourgeois milieu of the English novel (Edward Said would have approved). In the considerably less accomplished hands of Gurinder Chadha,

Bollywood's function is rather more conservative. Her rendering of *Pride and Prejudice* as *Bride and Prejudice* presents us with a settled and integrated world which celebrates the success of the wealthy and emphasizes the importance of sorority. In fact this has been the role of the Austen revival, to present a world not just in which there is a segregation of class but a segregation of gender. Rich boys on one side, rich girls on the other, the poor all delighting in their role as provider of meats to the rich man's estate. In *Bride and Prejudice* all classes celebrate the impending marriage of the wealthy daughters with a song of shameful banality.

Banality, however, is largely the point. The combination of big, loud, brash and witless works in a souped-up celeb-led culture. In *Mama Mia*, multiple Oscar-nominee and committed method-actress Meryl Streep renders a service to the audience roughly equivalent to the one that the Queen rendered her subjects in her televised address to the nation, undermining the Star system in favor of a kind of knockabout, girls-together romp through the dressing up box. Pierce Brosnan's desire to humiliate himself in the name of audience pleasure is perhaps even greater, the awfulness of his singing is exactly what's required, almost anyone could do better: a fumbling amateur-ishness, a lack of taking yourself seriously, an up for it, game-for-laughness is the supreme quality. Being enthusiastically shit is so much more comforting than serious, considered competence. An inverted sublimity is the aim; go to the film to feel how much more intelligent, how much more competent you are. You are the consumer, motor of history, what you consume must always be beneath you.

In *X Factor* Britain, we're all just a step away from celebrity and there is no higher accomplishment than being able to sing and dance. These capacities, along with that elusive x factor, detectable only by those of truly heightened sensibilities such as Simon Cowell and Cheryl Cole, are your tickets out of the most degrading of all personal situations, anonymity. *Mama Mia*, with its I-can-do-better-than-that pseudo-democratization of enticing blandness, plugs right into the notion that the distance between you and the supremely nondescript young couple in the movie is wafer thin. So close I'm practically already there. And mum and dad can be funky and passionate too. Your children will not view you with contempt and scorn, we can all live together in the great inter-generational Karaoke booth that is Britain Inc circa 2008. It's fitting that as the disparity between rich and poor increases to unprecedented levels and class mobility disappears, Bollywood becomes the model for Brit Feel-good.

# 8. Get out while you still can: *Sexy Beast* and *Morvern Callar*

In *Mamma Mia*, Greece provides a pleasantly rustic backdrop to the ongoing marriage and paternity crises of the central couple. The locals are a Greek chorus of smiling domestics and skipping peasants who simply occupy the position of local color, a spot of rustic charm. Greece is that Arcadia, "a place in the sun", the holiday home abroad, the fabulously cheap tumbledown old cottage on the sun-kissed shores that you can do up for tuppence and crow to your friends about. There are locals in the guise of servants, everything is conducted in English, no one is changed or liberated by the difference of the culture they inhabit, no-one views life differently or has their horizons widened, there is no becoming. It's a bright backdrop.

But in two of the best films of the past ten years, Jonathan Glazier's superlative *Sexy Beast* (2000) and Lynn Ramsay's *Morvern Callar* (2002), Spain, the country to which both central characters flee from the UK, functions on a much more ambiguous level. *Sexy Beast* may, on a surface level, be a generic Brit Gangster film and *Morvern Callar* a hip Indy-Arthouse piece, but there is an intriguing and fundamental congruence between the two. In both, Spain is a state of mind to which their central character, ex-East End bad-boy Gal Dove in the former, shy Supermarket shelf-stacker Morvern in the latter, have to adapt. What's significant here is that both characters are working class. The working class is traditionally vilified as the class who clog up the Costa del Sol with tacky bars and never learn the local tongue, whereas it's *Mama Mia*'s much more cosmopolitan middle-class milieu who are assumed to be the language speakers, the culture lovers, the ones who get involved. What's fundamental to the difference is need: the need to escape, an escape not just from the U.K. itself but from a certain restrictive Britishness.

## Costa del Sol

In *Sexy Beast*, Spain and England are both real locales within the film and also contradictory and warring elements within the central character Gal's psyche, just as his nemesis Don Logan is both a real figure and also a manifestation of everything within Gal that must be overcome so that he can be liberated fully and finally embrace the world of pleasure and get away from the destructive demands of Englishness.

*Sexy Beast* casts England as the Kingdom of Doom, the place to which you only return under pain of death. Gal's intense, erotic engagement with heat and light captures the very real English obsession with southern Spain and the Med as an enchanted realm where people really live, far from the damp and the gray, the oppressive social strictures and isolating, cramped family structures of the stoical, hedged English-way-of-death. A warm, emotive, physically expressive, unrestrained zone of rich libidinal and affective outpouring. This is where Gal has chosen to live, in his villa, with his lovely wife Dee-Dee, his surrogate Spanish son, his extended family of Aitch and Jackie. There is an early conflating of both Spain and the love that Gal has found with Dee-Dee during Gal's monologue on England, which is a kind of Cockney equivalent to Robinson's ruminations on England in *London*. Though of course unlike petit-bourgeoisie intellectual Robinson, who can at least extract a certain comforting frisson from his investigations into "the problem of England", for Gal Dove and for Morvern it is simply a problem to be avoided rather than aestheticized.

The first part of the monologue runs over a series of shots of Gal and his friends enjoying a barbecue:

People say, "Don't you miss it, Gal?"
"I say, "What? England? Nah, fuckin' place. It's a dump. Don't make me laugh. Grey, grimy, sooty. What a shithole. What a toilet. Every cunt with a long face, shufflin' about, moanin' or worried. No thanks, not for me."

The second part of the monologue – heard over a shot of Gal blowing a heart-shaped smoke ring toward Dee-Dee and the couple floating above the dark sierras in a passionate embrace – goes:

They say, "What's it like, then? Spain."
"And I'll say, "It's hot. Hot. Oh, it's fuckin' hot."
"Too hot?"
"Not for me. I love it."

There is a direct association of Spain, heat, Dee-Dee. The implication is that, while "Spain" might be too hot for some, that the intensity of pleasure and fulfillment that the satisfactions of a deep love bring may overwhelm or be unattainable to certain narrow English sensibilities, Gal is able to live with it.

In the hands of a less skillful, less subtle director it would be easy for *Sexy Beast*'s central characters to be grotesques. A little more distance from them, a little more pandering to middlebrow expectations, a touch more irony in the presentation and Gal, Jackie, Dee-Dee and Aitch with their gold rings, tans, beerguts, sangria and paella could easily be caricatures. The title sequence, soundtracked by the Stranglers' vulagrian anthem "Peaches" and its freeze frame shot of Winstone's crotch and prodigious gut sets up precisely those expectations, only to gradually subvert them. Glazier does this brilliantly. He makes his characters sympathetic not by appealing to our prejudices and sensibilities but by maintaining fidelity to theirs. The monologue sequence above is rendered largely in the non-realist language of advertising, and one of *Sexy Beast*'s most marked qualities is in its skillful interplay of the realist and hyperreal. The sausages on the Costa-del-crime and the swimming pool with two interlocked hearts may offend bourgeois taste but for Gal and Dee-Dee it is the stuff-of-dreams and Glazier renders it as such without irony. Whereas someone like Mike Leigh is incapable of depicting, or indeed imagining, the rituals and ambitions of the proles without the distance that lends itself to pathos, it's this affirmation of the characters' inner lives, a siding with the characters against (a certain section of) the audience that is a part of *Sexy Beast*'s sly subversion.

## Gal Dove

Gal's happiness is shattered by the arrival of his old partner in crime, Don Logan. His arrival, and the underwater tunneling job Gal is later forced to go through with, are foreshadowed in the film by a boulder crashing into Gal's swimming pool, narrowly missing him and cracking the link between the two interlocked hearts picked out in tiles on the floor of the pool.

The symbolism is obvious, even labored, but immediately *Sexy Beast*'s refusal to adopt one of the standard tropes of postmodern cinema, the it's-all-in-the-hero's-mind non-revelation, is evident. The boulder that narrowly misses Gal's head is both an event in his psyche and a real occurrence within his world. Whereas in *Fight Club*, for example, Tyler Durden doesn't actually exist, for Glazier, quite rightly, the people we know, the people to whom we cleave, do become part of us and do function as agents in the psyche. Hence Don, when he finally arrives, is both real and a part of Gal's mind. He can't simply be rendered as fantasmatic. The battle we have in our heads is with concrete figures whose discourse we've incorporated and who function as a variety of psychological equivalences, i.e. Don is both symbolically Gal's superego and also the person who stands as a superego agent within Gal's social field.

In *Sexy Beast*, what happens in your head is dependent on the world around you. You are the people you know, you are the place you come from. Whereas in *Fight Club* Edward Norton finally has to literally try and kill the other in his head before he can be brought on to love, with *Sexy Beast's* more dialogic, materialist take, the death of Don Logan is a collaborative effort. Each member of the group has a reason to despise Don but above and beyond this, with Gal partly incapacitated, his friends must take on a role in helping him overcome and destroy Don, even the Spanish boy who helps out attempts it, but it's finally Dee-Dee who manages to pull the trigger. It's a kind of group therapy, an act of love on Gal's behalf, and this is partly where *Sexy Beast's* other main strength lies, it is unashamed in talking about and believing in love.

### Don Logan

"I won't let you be happy, why should I?"

Don's doubleness is emphasized at the film's end: dead and buried beneath the restored hearts at the bottom of the pool, he nonetheless maintains an immaterial half-life, still talking to Gal, who now, within his own mind, has finally overcome him and is capable of telling him to shut up, much to Don's disgruntlement.

Don is, in his own way, a master of language and it's

precisely this that makes him the only genuinely menacing villain in recent British film. Don's mastery is primarily over the language of others, alive to every nuance and inflection in their speech, the faintest hint of an insult or a refusal, the smallest of "insinuendos".

Look, Don...
Look, Don?
It's like this.
Like what?
I'm... retired.
Are ya?
'Fraid so. I haven't... not got lots of money. I got enough. I'd do anything not to offend you, but I can't take part. I'm not really up to it.
Not up to it?
No, I'm not.
I see.
I'd be useless.
Useless.
I would be.
In what way?
In every fuckin' way.
Why are you swearin'? I'm not swearin'

And:

What's that mean?–
What?
That stupid nodding you're doing. Is this a fuck-off, Gal?
No, course not.
Are you saying no?
No.
Is that what you're saying?

Not exactly.

What are you saying?

I'm just saying ... Thanks and all that, thanks for thinking of me, but I've got to turn this opportunity down.

No, you've got to turn this opportunity yes.

I'm not match fit.

You seem all right to me.

Not really.

You look fine Do the job.

What?

Do the job.

No, Don.

Yes.

No.

Yes.

I can't.

Can.

I can't.

Don't do this.

Do what? What am I doin'?!

This.

This? This what?

It's not only Don's tensed alertness to Gal's speech that's frightening, it's also the jackknifing instability of his own discourse. By turns cajoling and punishing, consoling and caustic, there is no solid ground with Don, no predictable syntactic chains that allow for a proper presentation of your own discourse. Not only this, but the wild imagistic absurdity of Don's language, together with its playground name-calling and absurd malapropisms, throw both Gal and the audience into a kind of freefall, half terrifying, half thrilling.

Talk to me, Gal. I'm here for you. I'm a good listener.

What can I say? I've said it all. I'm retired.

Shut up! Cunt. You louse. You got some fuckin' neck. Retired? Fuck off, you're revolting.

Your fuckin' suntan, you're like leather. Like a leather man. You could make a fuckin' suitcase. You look like a fat crocodile, fat bastard. You look like fuckin' Idi Amin.

State of you. You should be ashamed of yourself. Who d'you think you are?

King of the castle? Cock of the walk?

Finest of all is Don's threat to Aitch, a hilariously inventive and disturbing crescendo of twisted, playground poetics.

You fucking Dr White honkin' jam-rag fucking spunk-bubble!

You keep lookin' at me, I'll put you in the fucking ground.

### The rabbit

Don isn't alone in his cave under the swimming pool of course, he's also joined by the movie's symbol of death (drive), something that's best summed up by the term Giant Death Rabbit. The Rabbit menaces Gal in a dream sequence, and in his later meeting with crime kingpin Teddy Bass the sequence is partially replayed, reintegrating it from the imaginary realm into the film's real-world frame brilliantly. In an early sequence both Aitch and Gal's surrogate son fail to kill the rabbits they are hunting due to problems with their guns, and soon the Rabbit has returned in monstrous form to symbolize the world that Gal has left behind – the world of crime and its transgressive delights. Don Logan knows who Gal really is, what drives animate him. "It's not about money with us, is it? It's the charge, the bolt, the buzz. The sheer fuck-offness, right?"

Gal's early inspection of the boulder and his emerging from the pool to find Dee-Dee waiting is echoed later in his being dragged up out of the bath into Teddy Bass's smoking underworld. England is an infernal realm, the realm of the Id and the drives, the realm of death, over which the satanic Teddy Bass, "Mr Black Magic himself", presides, and of which Don Logan is merely a minion. There's a wormhole beneath the London streets that leads the viewer back to Spain, to the moment of Don's murder, fixing his interment and the refilling of the pool to the breakthrough into the vault that brings an end to Gal's commitment to Teddy Bass. He gets a desultory fiver and at last he can return.

## Morvern calling

It would be churlish not to acknowledge Lynn Ramsey's *Morvern Callar* as a masterpiece, one of the few that British cinema has produced in the last ten years and a massive extension on both her short films and the widely praised debut *Ratcatcher*.

Adapted from Alan Warner's novel of the same name, the film centers on Morvern, a supermarket worker in Scotland whose boyfriend commits suicide, leaving her a compilation tape to listen to and the unpublished manuscript of his novel. She sends the novel to a publisher, passing it off as her own work, disposes of her boyfriend's body and later embarks on a holiday to Spain with her best friend Lana. In Spain she becomes more distant in her attitude toward both Lana and the pleasure of a typical Brits-abroad holiday package, striking out on her own to explore the country. While there she discovers that she is to receive a huge advance for the novel and returns to Scotland briefly, offering Lana the chance to come with her. Lana refuses and Morvern leaves alone.

## The central character

In some senses Morvern Callar is not a "character" at all: though she is central to the narrative she is also radically de-centered. Morvern is, by the standards of conventional heroines (or central characters) both inexpressive and passive: she's a cipher of sorts, it would be hard even at the film's end to sum up her attributes, to say "who she is". Morvern certainly undergoes a transformation, and in this sense the film is about her "journey", but there is no heroic narrative of struggle against adversity, this is not a triumph of the will as such but rather a vision of the mysterious alchemy of experience in which, unbeknownst to or even against ourselves we find that incrementally and often fundamentally we have changed.

Samantha Morton's casting is integral to Morvern Caller's success: there is a blank, fetal quality to her face that suits her to the role of ingénue or otherwise otherworldly characters, hence her surprising but inspired casting as a telepath (floating in a womb-like tank) in Spielberg's *Minority Report* (2002). In *Morvern Callar*, Morton's childlike features and affective blankness is used as a way of pushing the viewers attention out and away from the nominal heroine herself and onto peripheral factors, the world at hand. On the simplest level Ramsay's commitment is to showing and not telling, to cinema as a visual medium, and against much of the tradition of filmed theater in British cinema.

## The sense of touch

Throughout *Morvern Callar* there is a repeated focus on Morvern's hands, on the sense of touch. The film opens in the aftermath of her boyfriend's suicide, Morvern lying on the floor beside him and stroking his dead flesh, his cut wrists. Except for a brief interlude at a house rave when she twines her fingers around another raver's as they lie together on the bed, everything she touches in Scotland is redolent of death. She strokes the dead leaves on the plant at Lana's grandmother's house, pokes at the maggot writhing in the carrot in the supermarket where she works. It's only after she has buried her boyfriend that she begins to intuit the possibility of a new sensual relation to the world, stroking the buds on a bush, immersing her hands in the thaw water, touching the grubs that are struggling back to life from below the surface of the ice and cold. For a certain period of time in Spain her hands disappear. Here she is all watchful face; this is an interstitial period, between two selves, in which the affective and physical dimensions of life are in abeyance. Once she has rejected Lana and struck out on her own, Morvern re-engages with her hands, painting her nails again and holding her hand up to the window to admire them in the glare of the Spanish sunlight. The final shot before Morvern returns to what seems to be the perpetual night of Scotland is of her fingers buried in the red earth of Spain and an ant crawling over her hand.

In some ways this symbolizes the passage through grief, though it can't be read merely as such. Morvern's change is figured in several ways, firstly through the use of color. Immediately after her boyfriend's suicide she is dressed entirely in black, a gothic siren who raises her skirts to reveal her suspenders and stockings to a passing boat. Slowly, red begins to take over as her dominant color. From a red hat at first to – once she has disposed of her boyfriend – a red sweater. In the Costa del Sol she wears a red dress and toward the end of the film in the same sequence where she paints her nails, puts on a bright red, leaf-pattern dress before she meets the literary agents who will make her rich.

The insects play a part in this process of transfiguration too, from the maggots in Scotland to the cockroach, a harbinger of death that leads her from her apartment in Spain to the room of the young man whose mother has just died and her final engagement with a certain form of death-driven pleasure. The sequence in the hotel room with the boy, in which they take Ecstasy and make love, begins with Morvern's offer to tell him about her stepmother's funeral and ends with a bright-eyed hyper-alert Morvern realizing that she must get out of the English zone, head deeper inland. In doing so she passes through the celebrations in a Spanish village. As she leaves she sees two children playing a game with the same insect that has lead her to the boy's door in which it is crushed with a stone. Later the ants crawl over her hand as she smiles. Something has been conquered. These three images or passages of transfiguration run side by side in *Morvern Callar*, but perhaps the most important and the most telling in broadening out the films attempt to offer a passage through Britishness rather than just an escape from Britain is in its use of music.

### The sense of hearing

Morvern is left a tape by her boyfriend who, apart from being a suicidal but brilliant novelist, also seems to have had achingly hip taste in music, even if he is overly fixated on Can. The cassette he gives to Morvern also functions largely as the soundtrack to the film, except for some Flamenco which we might assume is coming from the taxi driver's radio as they head into the heart of Andalusia and some music at the rave Morvern ducks out of in Spain. The use of sound is another way in which the film suggests a passage through experience. The movement of the music in the sequences up to the burial of Morvern's boyfriend goes through three stages. First it is heard on the soundtrack, then, at a lower volume, in Morvern's headphones, before it finally disappears altogether as Morvern clicks the tape off. There is a movement here of assimilation, processing and sublimation.

In a famous sequence Morvern turns up for work listening

to the Lee Hazlewood and Nancy Sinatra version of "Some Velvet Morning" and the enormous, glowing signs for fruit take on a hint of the otherworldly. Something fundamental to the British obsession with music is got at here in this idea that music has the power to transform the banality of the everyday. The expansive sweep of "Some Velvet Morning"'s acid-infused vistas and the Technicolor fruit foreshadow Morvern's ecstatic encounter with Southern Spain once she has got away from the British habits of boredom, drugs and fucking the pain away.

There is also the scene where Morvern buries her boyfriend, in which by pressing stop on her Walkman she turns off the soundtrack itself, suggesting a direct control over her environment, a surpassing. The next sequence is the trip to Spain (the idea itself has been prefigured in the postcard on the fridge that Morvern glances at in the ruined kitchen after the house party), in which Morvern must again move through an arc of overcoming. This overcoming, this rejection or mini-destitution is of rave itself and what rave stands for and stands in for. As mentioned earlier, in Spain, Morvern is watchful. She watches the drunk tourists play-fighting on the balcony and throwing water and toilet paper over each other. The next day the camera holds on the odd faces of the couple who have been made to strip and wear each other's clothes in a party game and even Lana has taken on a certain distance. Later, in the toilet, as the boys babble about a mythical super-club that a friend hasn't left for weeks, Morvern is fixated on the half-melted face of an E'd–up girl in black eyeliner stuck to the wall. The next morning, as she decides to leave, the question from the boy Lana is in bed with is "Do you want a pill?" A question met with a look of disbelief.

Just prior to this there is a rave sequence which is revisited as the film's coda. The sequence, with its extreme close up on

Morvern's face fading in and out of darkness in the flashing light, recalls the opening sequence in which Morvern curls fetally on the floor beside her dead boyfriend in the pulsing lights of the Christmas tree, the image again fading to black, then back in again. In this way the death drive is related to the quest for oblivion in rave. The coda, in which Morvern leaves Scotland to return to Spain, is a symbolic sequence in which she walks through the rave wearing headphones and listening to the Mama and Papas' song of renunciation, *To the One I love*. The track is again presented first as soundtrack, then in the headphones until, in the final cut to black we hear the tape click off. There is clearly a social as well as a psychological dimension in this passage.

### *The Isle of the dead*

Morvern's life in Scotland is figured by the image of the white grub writhing in the carrot. The camera pulls up and away from the shot of her hands toward the bright supermarket lights, a movement echoed in the two gestures up to the sky in the film, the first made by Lana's grandmother when Morvern visits her, pointing wordlessly out of the window as the snow falls, the second made by Morvern to the taxi driver who is to take her up to the village where the celebration is taking place. It is also repeated in the final shot in which Morvern sweeps up and back out of the rosy, womb-like darkness of the rave and off camera.

In the final moment of the film Morvern is now in some new space, where she has traversed her grief, and with it a peculiarly British attachment to misery. There is an overcoming here of the fear of any ecstatic experience not initiated by drugs and the embarrassment about any collective expression not mediated by the culture industry (in some ways the gang violence of football films and the national hysteria evident in *The Queen* shadow an English longing for collective ecstatic ritual, as does the nostalgia for rave). Lana is in a kind of idyll of poverty, a littleness of experience and expectation, a comfy nook in which the friends can take Ecstasy, work in the supermarket and hang out with the same reliable faces in the pub. Lana doesn't want to go back to Spain and is hostile to Morvern's having gone off the beaten track, away from the British Zone there. Spain is temperamentally unsuitable to her, she prefers to stay, as Teddy Bass does, as Don Logan does, in the Land of Night. "I like it here," she tells Morvern before she leaves for good. "It's the same crapness everywhere so stop dreaming" (echoing *Shallow Grave*'s cynicism about cities). Don Logan's first words on arriving in Spain are "I'm sweating like a cunt", in contrast to Gal Dove's blissful opening monologue on the heat.

The quietly visionary element in Ramsay's work is the rejection of several defensive positions (the idyll; the need to be "creative"; the half-satisfying, half-stultifying dwelling on the problem of England that provides sustenance to the psycho-geographers; the desire to assimilate upward a la Renton; the escapism of sticking to drugs) in the name of some new, unenvisionable way of living, an intercultural, expansive self that as yet resists clear figuration. Only what it has been and what it must escape can be adequately represented. The film begins with darkness and suicide and ends with darkness and rebirth, a different traversing to that found in Boyle's films. There is no reality to return to, only the void in which a new self can incubate. This is the anti-therapeutic element in the film; neither a refit to reality nor a liberal suspension of judgment is offered as pseudo-salve to alienation, instead there is simply a work of transformation to be undertaken. Morvern's boyfriend's injunction to her is "Be Brave". There is work to be done both outside and in and though the outcome is uncertain, unimaginable, life, finally, is on the side of this endeavor. The question posed at the start of

Terrence Malick's *The Thin Red Line* seems particularly appropriate to *Morvern Callar* and its representation of Britishness. "Is this darkness in you too? Have you passed through this night?"

Pass through it you must. Be brave. This is *Morvern Callar's* message.

Contemporary culture has eliminated both the concept of the public and the figure of the intellectual. Former public spaces – both physical and cultural – are now either derelict or colonized by advertising. A cretinous anti-intellectualism presides, cheerled by expensively educated hacks in the pay of multinational corporations who reassure their bored readers that there is no need to rouse themselves from their interpassive stupor. The informal censorship internalized and propagated by the cultural workers of late capitalism generates a banal conformity that the propaganda chiefs of Stalinism could only ever have dreamt of imposing. Zer0 Books knows that another kind of discourse – intellectual without being academic, popular without being populist – is not only possible: it is already flourishing, in the regions beyond the striplit malls of so-called mass media and the neurotically bureaucratic halls of the academy. Zer0 is committed to the idea of publishing as a making public of the intellectual. It is convinced that in the unthinking, blandly consensual culture in which we live, critical and engaged theoretical reflection is more important than ever before.